EN

"Despite the evident abuse, hurt and pain, this book is an embodiment of love. It displays lives being changed through very simple acts, while at times experiencing complex difficulties. True love unfolds through each page. It triumphs over every act of selfish love, betrayal, rejection and exclusion. This book rehearses the power of "LOVE and "LETTING GO!!!! It's a great eye-opener!"

Ms. Felicia Grant

"You just see my glory, but you don't know my story." We must understand in life everyone that is experiencing God's glory has a story to be told. Don't be ashamed to tell your story, it might save someone else's life."

Pastor Prenis Edmond

"Once I started to read this book I could not put it down. Dianna was able to put on paper what others would want to hide. Her determination not to let the abuse she suffered bring her down was what impressed me the most. She truly understands what God's love and grace really are. I am blessed to have a woman of such strength and resilience in my life and one that I call friend."

Mrs. Pamela Huber

Editor's Notes

I have to say it has been my extreme honor and pleasure to read your story. Through every twist and turn of your life's journey, I went with you. I felt your pain, heard your cries and saw so vividly the scenes you painted so clearly. So many times it wasn't you anymore, but me that I saw.

I can't tell you how our lives parallel so closely. Just when you think "oh you don't know what I've been through", God shows you that you're not alone in your situation.

Oh, how I know what it is to yell at the height of your voice but no one hears or sees you. I know only too well how the deep ache of deliberately being inflicted with pain and mistreatment feels; and how badly it hurts when it's by people who are supposed to love and take care of you.

You definitely spoke to my hidden places. You uncovered some issues that I haven't dealt with completely and helped me to admit that I'm still angry about some things that have been done to me. More than anything, you've shown me how to get free; truly free. For this I sincerely thank you.

It is my belief and hope that your book will lead readers to identify with their hurt places; and seek the true healing God has available for them.

Phyllis M. Bridges, Editor

DIANNA KNOX COOPER

Hope of Vision
Publishing
Bridgeport, Connecticut

Hated Without A Cause

All scripture references and quotations in this book are taken from the King James Version of the Bible.

Hope of Vision Publishing a division of HOV, LLC.
www.Hopeofvisionpublishing.com
hopeofvision@gmail.com

Cover Design: Hope of Vision Designs
Editor: Phyllis M. Bridges
Back cover Photo Credit: J. Michael Seward, Imagination Nation
                    Email: jmichaelseward@hotmail.com

Contact the Author at:
Dianna Knox Cooper
Email: ladyditheauthor@gmail.com

For more information about special discounts for bulk purchases, please contact
Email: ladyditheauthor@gmail.com or www.hopeofvisionpublishing.com.

ISBN 978-0-9884773-5-3
Library of Congress Control Number: 2013940355

10   9   8   7   6   5   4   3   2   1

Printed in the United States of America

DEDICATION

This book is dedicated in memory of
my maternal grandmother, my beloved mother,
and my baby brother.

ACKNOWLEDGEMENTS

I would like to thank Father God, my LORD and Savior Jesus Christ and my comforter, The Holy Spirit for choosing me, saving me, loving me, guiding me and keeping me close through all of my trials, hurts, tribulations and pains.

To my husband, of 23 years…although we may not have lived in the same house for all 23 years, you have always been there for me whenever I needed you. No matter what time of day or night I called, you never failed to come see about me. Thank you for putting up with me and my difficult attitudes and demands I placed on you. Thank you for loving me in spite of; not because of. Thank you for the many times when I said to you, "I want a divorce!" you said to me, "Till death do us part." I love you.

To my children, I thank God for blessing me with you. You have brought so much joy and laughter to my heart and soul. Proverbs 13:22a says, *A good man leaveth an inheritance to his children's children:* This is for you. I love you to life.

To my beloved sisters, mere words cannot express the love I have for you. You were my "first" children. We have been in this thing together from the very beginning. As it says in Ecclesiastes 4:12 *And if one prevail against him, two shall withstand him; and a threefold cord is not quickly broken.* We are that threefold cord. I love you both.

To my nieces and nephews, I love you like my own children.

To my girlfriends (you know who you are), I thank you all for your lifetime friendships. I thank you for letting me vent, cry, complain, cuss, laugh or whatever I needed to do, without judging me.

To my father, thank you for being my first pastor and introducing me to the Word of God.

To my mother-in-law, thank you for continuing to encourage and persuade me to love my enemies no matter what.

To my pastor, thank you for being real with me at all times and teaching me what true beauty is.

To my spiritual father and mother, thank you for being you.

To my extended family, I love each and every one of you beyond measure.

To my adopted mom, thank you for your never ending true love and support for me and my sisters.

To my sister from another mother, (you know who you are), you know it all; the good, the bad and the ugly, yet you still love me.

To the photographer...Thank you so much for capturing my "beauty" and helping me to "see" it for the first time in my life.

Thanks to EVERYONE who made this book possible.

CONTENT

EPIGRAGH

"Let not them that are mine enemies wrongfully rejoice over me: neither let them wink with the eye that hate me without a cause." Ps. 35:19

"They that hate me without a cause are more than the hairs of mine head: they that would destroy me, being mine enemies wrongfully, are mighty: then I restored that which I took not away." Ps 69:4

"But this cometh to pass, that the word might be fulfilled that is written in their law, THEY HATED ME WITHOUT A CAUSE." John 15:25

PREFACE

"And we know that all things work together for good to them that love God, to them who are the called according to his purpose. For who He did foreknow, He also did predestinate to be conformed to the image of His Son, that He might be the firstborn among many brethren. Moreover whom He did predestinate, them He also called: and who He called, them He also justified: and whom He justified, them He also glorified. What shall we then say to these things? If God be for us, who can be against us? He that spared not His own Son, but delivered Him up for us all, how shall He not with Him also freely give us all things? Who shall lay anything to the charge of God's elect? It is God that justifieth. Who is he that condemneth? It is Christ that died, yea rather, that is risen again, who is even at the right hand of God, who also maketh intercession for us. Who shall separate us from the love of Christ? Shall tribulation, or distress, or persecution, or famine or nakedness, or peril, or sword? As it is written, for thy sake we are killed all the day long; we are accounted as sheep for the slaughter. Nay, in all these things we are more than conquerors through Him that loved us. For I am persuaded, that neither death, nor life, nor angels, nor principalities, nor powers, nor things present, nor things to come. Nor height, nor depth, nor any other creature, shall be able to separate us from the love of God, which is in Christ Jesus our LORD," Rom. 8:28-39

As I was reading and typing this portion of scripture, it brought tears to my eyes. I have read it many times before, but it never quite touched me like this before. In fact, the only portion I ever got anything out of in times past was verse 28. I'm sure you are very familiar with that verse also.

But according to Timothy, we must always, *"Study to show thyself approved unto God, a workman that needeth not to be ashamed, rightly dividing the Word of Truth."* 2 Timothy 2:15. I now realize that God chose me before the foundation of the world and everything that I have gone through in my life was meant for my good. And the very same thing holds true for you.

I took the scripture from Isaiah 49:1, 5 and made it read just for me... "The LORD hath called me (Dianna) from the womb; from the bowels of my mother hath he made mention of my name (Dianna). And now, saith the LORD that formed me (Dianna) from the womb to be His servant."

To protect identities, no one's name, other than my own, will be used in this book.

As it once was with the Israelites, this is my 40th year......

FORWARD

Once you have met Dianna Cooper, you won't forget her. Dianna's vitality, intelligence, hard work and wit are just a few of the things that set her apart from the rest of us. I have been fortunate enough to work with Dianna, and even more fortunate to count her as a friend.

When she coordinated our successful United Way fundraising campaign a few years ago, all of us got to know her better when she shared the story of the fire that destroyed her family's home and all of their possessions. She told the story without a trace of self-pity, and focused instead on her gratitude for her family's safety and the help she received.

When she asked me to read her book, the same strength and bravery were obvious. After living through some of the most horrific events a young girl (or anyone else for that matter) could endure, instead of dwelling on self-pity or anger and bitterness, Dianna focused on her spiritual growth in God. She focused on making peace with her past and with the people who allowed those events to happen.

Lots of us avoid thinking about the awful things that can happen in our lives. Maybe we're scared that letting those thoughts into our minds will somehow let the events into our lives. Or perhaps, we feel powerless because we can't undo bad things, or prevent them.

Dianna's book made me uncomfortable: not the writing or the subject, but the fact that someone I know and think so highly of had to endure those things. It is surely a tribute to her strength and resilience that she not only endured but grew, and is willing to share her pain to help others endure and grow.

Perhaps you know someone who has been victimized as Dianna was, or you have been victimized yourself, or you simply care about others as our Maker commanded us. Whatever your perspective, I hope after reading Dianna's book you will feel you know her, and can use the experience, strength and hope she shares to make something positive happen in the world. You surely won't forget her, or the story she so generously and bravely shares.

Susan Hagemeyer

INTRODUCTION

Did you suffer abuse as a child?

Did you suffer abuse as a teenager?

Have you suffered abuse as an adult?

Have you suffered spousal abuse?

Have you inflicted pain on others?

Is your past ruining your future?

Do you want to be healed?

Know you are not alone; God is with you as He has been all the time. He is the Healer of all wounds.

This story is about the first 39 years of my life. It is about the abuse I endured from an early age; during my teenage years and my adult married life.

The pangs of my past controlled my life for 35 years. I was a very angry, bitter woman; I hid my feelings with a big smile every day of my life.

But one day, I received a WORD from God that was just for me, at the right time that started my healing process.

As you read through these pages, see me as that little girl growing and blossoming into the Woman of God I am today.

And now, I share my story with you.....

CHAPTER 1
MY FAMILY

It was the tradition of my maternal grandmother's family for the grandmother to either help or raise the oldest grandchild of each of her children. So being the firstborn to my mom and dad, it was quite natural for me to go and live with my grandmother and grandfather. I was raised by my grandparents for the first four years of my life. I remember my grandmother teaching me The Lord's Prayer. Every night before we went to bed, she would sit down in her rocking chair in front of the fireplace, place me on her lap and read the Bible to me. Once she finished she would take me to the bedroom and tell me to get down on my knees and repeat The Lord's Prayer after her. Now that I reflect back on that, I realize more than ever, that I was truly handpicked and chosen by God from the beginning. He used my grandmother to teach me about Him at a very early age. I thank Him for that.

My mom and dad went on to have three more children after me, two girls and a boy. When my mom gave birth to my brother (her youngest child), the doctor informed her that if she were to get pregnant again, she could possibly lose her life. That is exactly what happened to her five months later. She became pregnant, miscarried and died. She actually died as my dad was transporting her to the hospital. My mom didn't believe in birth control and was a firm believer that women were put on the earth to bear children. She was 26 years old at the time of her death on July 18, 1974. When my mom died, I was four years old; my sisters were only one and two years old and my baby brother was five months old. She was buried on July 26, 1974.

When my mom died, I'm sure I missed her, but I don't remember feeling a loss for her like someone would feel who lost their mom. Because I didn't live with my mom and dad, in my little four year old mind, I still had my *"Mom"* my grandmother. Immediately after the death of my mom, my grandmother and grandfather became the caregivers, not only to me, but to my siblings as well.

Four months later, my life changed forever. On November 11, 1974, my dad remarried and a few days later, took me and my siblings away from my *"Mom"* and my *"Dad"*, our grandparents. I was devastated. As a little child, I remember the day quite well when my dad came to take us to our new home. That was a very sad day in my life. My grandmother did not want to let us go. I didn't want to go. In fact, as soon as I realized what was going on, I ran into my bedroom and hid under the bed. After many shed tears by my grandmother and me, pleading with my father to let us stay, my grandfather persuaded my grandmother to let us go. Even though we lived in the very same town as our grandparents, we rarely saw them again after that day.

My dad and my "birth" mom owned a three bedroom, one and half bath single-wide mobile home, but for some reason, my dad chose to move us into my step-mother's house. It had three bedrooms and one bathroom. Once we got to our new home, my siblings and I were then introduced to our step-brothers and step-sisters, two boys and two girls. The two boys were older than me (not exactly sure of their ages, but I believe my oldest step-brother was at least five years older than me) and as for the girls, one was almost a year younger than me and the baby girl was only five months old. My dad and step-mother would later have two more children together, both girls.

For the first couple of months after we moved in, all of us stayed in my step-mother's house, the boys shared a room, the girls shared a room and the two babies, (my little brother and my baby step-sister) slept in a baby bed in my parent's bedroom. A short time later, my dad had his single-wide mobile home moved and pulled into the back yard of my step-mother's house up to the back porch. Let me give you a clearer picture of how the mobile home was setup. The back door of the mobile home opened up to the porch, which led into the back door of the house. The porch was not covered; it was just cement with a few steps leading off of it. The mobile home covered the steps that led off the porch. The front door of the mobile home faced the dirt road that was behind the house; it was later paved. We were not allowed to use the front door of the mobile home. My dad took the steps that originally belonged to the front door of the mobile home and placed them beside the porch of the house so that we could walk down them at any time. He had the electricity turned on in the mobile home and then he moved me and my two sisters into it. From that moment on, at the age of five, I became my sisters' *"Mother."* Although my little brother stayed in the house, I became his mother also. I had to bathe him, dress him, change his diapers, etc.

Even though there were one and a half bathrooms in the mobile home, we had no running water in it. We had to go in the house to use the bathroom or take a bath. We were not allowed to take showers; my step-mother made that perfectly clear to us. She said that taking showers would make the water bill go up. So, my oldest step-sister, who is younger than me, would take her bath first. Instead of her letting her water out of the bathtub when she finished taking her bath, we all had to bathe in the same bath water. Yes, my sisters and I would each take turns bathing in the dirty bathwater of the person before us. Most times we used the same bath cloth to bathe with and the same towel to dry off. The last person to take her bath was responsible for cleaning the bathtub.

We were allowed to stay in the house during the day, but when it was time to go to bed, out to the mobile home me and my sisters had to go. The house was locked up at night, so if we had to use the bathroom in the middle of the night, we had to go outside. It was awful. Sometimes the moon would be shining and the pathway around the mobile home could be seen clearly. Other times, it would be pitch dark and I would have to keep my hand on the mobile home to feel my way around it. I can't remember ever being scared, it just became the norm. I can see myself, as I am typing this, having to go outside and walk around the mobile home to urinate. Although it wasn't safe at all, it would have been safer to just go outside the mobile home, walk off the porch and urinate right there. We did that at first, but when our step-mother discovered that, she told us not to do it because we were making it smell like urine around her door. I type this now and I laugh, not because it is funny, but in total disbelief!

I had no choice but to grow up and completely lose my childhood. At the time, I didn't realize what was going on. I thought it was just the normal way of life, I guess. To me, it was either sink or swim. I had to learn how to do my sisters hair and wash our clothes. I was allowed to use the washing machine in the house, but not the dryer. I had to hang our clothes out on the clothesline every season of the year. I remember during the winter time, when I went to take the clothes in, they would be frozen stiff. I wasn't allowed to use the iron at all; it was another thing my step-mother told me would make the light bill go up too high.

As I stated earlier, the mobile home had three bedrooms. One of course was a master bedroom that had the full bathroom attached to it. The decision was made that my sisters and me were to share the smallest bedroom. I later found out the reason for that was, when my step-mother's family (her sisters and their families) would come to visit, they would have somewhere to stay.

During the winter time, we were only allowed to have the heater on just before we went to bed and right after we got up to get dressed for school. It was not allowed to stay on during the day or at night when we went to sleep. My sisters and I snuggled up really close to each other at night to keep warm. We would take turns and often fight over who would get to sleep in the middle because we knew that was the warmest spot in the bed. Most times it would be so cold in the mobile home that we could breathe and see "smoke" coming out of our mouths.

Every Saturday, my parents would go shopping and leave all of us children in the care of our oldest step-brother. He treated me and my siblings very ugly. He picked on us, hit and beat us; we were terrified of him. One incident, I remember quite clearly and it still disturbs me to this very day. I was in the bathroom in the house getting ready to change my little brother's diaper; back then we used

23

cloth diapers. My oldest step-brother came into the bathroom where I was and purposely turned off the light and closed the door so I couldn't see what I was doing. There wasn't a window in the bathroom, which made it almost pitch black in there except for the light that was coming from up under the door. I reached up and turned the light switch back on. Once again, he opened the door and turned the light back off. So in the dark, I proceeded to change my brother's diaper. I put my fingers inside of the diaper so that I would not stick him with the diaper pin. When I opened the bathroom door to go out, my step-brother made me unpin the diaper and go back in the dark bathroom to re-pin the diaper. This went on for about two more times. As I sat there in the dark one final time, I asked my five-year old self, "Why does he keep doing that? What does he want me to do?" I came to the conclusion that my step-brother must have wanted me to stick my baby brother with the diaper pin. I took the diaper pin and stuck my baby brother, not hard enough to pierce his skin, but just enough to make him cry out and to confirm my thoughts. I had to be correct in my thinking because just as I did that, my step-brother opened up the bathroom door, turned the light on and walked away.

Although I couldn't see it, understand it or reason with it back then, God was working in my life even as a child. He was making and molding me to become the woman I am today. Sure in my adult life, I have oftentimes asked God, "Why?" I wondered why he allowed me to go through such a traumatic experience of losing two mothers within months of each other in my early childhood. Why did my dad take me and my siblings from the warm comforting home of our loving grandparents only to isolate us from him and our new family as well? How could a man who called himself a "Man of God" do that to his children? Why did God allow my mom to die? Why didn't my dad use protection to prevent my mom from getting pregnant again? All these questions and many more I have asked God over and over again. Well, the Lord knew the plans He had for my life even before I was born. The enemy had a plan also to abort my destiny; he was doing everything in his power to do just that. I believe what God said when he spoke to the Prophet Jeremiah in Jer.

24

1:5, *"Before I formed thee in the belly I knew thee; and before thou camest forth out of the womb I sanctified thee, and I ordained thee a prophet unto the nations."* I now understand that when a person is chosen by God and He puts His anointing on his or her life, the greater the tribulations one must go through to fulfill the whole Will of God. I went through all that pain and suffering for someone else, not just for me. I had to experience it so God could deliver me and in turn help deliver someone else, someone like you.

Right now, you may not feel it or even see your way out from underneath the darkness of your pain. I am a living witness that God can and will deliver you. You have to give it ALL to Him and remember that He has allowed or is allowing this to happen for a reason.

Since I have been grown, I took the opportunity to ask both my dad and my step-mother why they made the choice to lock us out of the house and put me and my two little sisters out in the mobile home to sleep at night. My step-mother quickly replied that it was my daddy's choice. I then asked her why wasn't the choice made to put the two older boys out in the mobile home instead of us. She responded that she would never make her boys give up their room. My dad then stated to me that he let his wife rule her own house. The division between our "so-called family" is undeniable. It was there from the beginning and it is still very present to this day that I am typing these pages.

Even to this very day, I don't understand my dad's response to me. But I do know one thing for sure: God has ALWAYS been in control of my life.

(I had always thought that my dad had gotten married a year and four months after my mom passed. It was only after I was older and asked him about it, did I realize that it was only four months after my mom's death that he was remarried. I made the statement to him that he didn't even give my mother's body time to get cold. His response to me was, "I could have gotten married the next day if

I wanted to." The very moment he spoke those words to me, my heart began to feel sorrowful. I felt that my dad must not have truly loved my mother. I would also like to add that during those four months, he was engaged to marry someone else, broke up with her and married my current step-mother.

I am not sharing my life to degrade anyone, but I want you, the reader, to hear my story and see me as that little five year old girl having to care for my siblings with no one to really care for me. I had no mother, no grandmother...just me. So from that point on, I put myself last and I still do to this very day. Oh, but I'm so grateful to God, that all the while, He put me first. For even before I was conceived in my mother's womb, He knew me; before I was born He sanctified me. I was predestined by God, called and justified by Him; as well was all that I have endured and have yet to encounter. Yes, every one of my days He predestined to work to my good. What an awesome God we serve!)

CHAPTER 2
My Father the Pastor

My dad and step-mother both left the church they were attending and started their own ministry. I am not sure what happened or their reason for that decision. My dad became the "Pastor" for our family. As far back as I can remember, my step-mother has confessed to be a "Holy Ghost Filled", "Fire Baptized", "Woman of God."

In the beginning, my dad used to hold his weekly services in the living room of the mobile home where my sisters and I stayed at night. I remember several times some of our relatives came and participated. My dad would have service on Sunday mornings and Friday nights.

Shortly after that, he moved the services to an old wooden house in the country that he renovated into a church. I think he may have been renting the old house for the purpose of it being a church. The church had no running water and no working bathroom in it.

We had church every Sunday morning and prayer meeting on Friday nights. At first, the congregation consisted only of us, the family. Then my step-mother's sister started attending. My grandmother (my mom's mother) and few of her friends would visit occasionally.

We would have Sunday school, followed by a small break in between, and then go into Sunday service. My step-mother would do devotional service and sing most of the songs. My father played the guitar, my oldest step-brother played the drums and my step-mother played her tambourine.

On Sundays, it seemed that we were in church all day long. My step-mother would bring snacks for herself, such as a banana or crackers, to eat during the break between Sunday school and church. She also brought something to drink with her. I am almost sure that she shared what she had with her children. I know one thing: my sisters and I never got a snack or anything to eat until after we got home well into the afternoon.

My step-siblings always had breakfast before we left for church. I will explain why in a later chapter. But my sisters and I had to go the whole morning and afternoon without eating. I used to get sick at church from being so hungry. I would start throwing up gastric juices because that was the only thing in my stomach.

During church, if my sisters or I dozed off to sleep, my step-mother would wake us and make us stand up during the entire service. If we were at church during the night service, it wasn't enough for her to make us stand up; she would make us go outside and stand on the porch in the dark. There was not a porch light at the church.

In my opinion, my father was what one would call a "legalistic" preacher. He was very strict. I mean, he lived straight by the Bible according to his understanding of it. His introduction of God to me was not pleasant at all. He preached the fear of God into me at a very early age. I thought of God as being very angry and not loving at all. It was as if I did anything wrong it was an abomination to God; and He would be very angry with me and punish me for the least little thing. I cannot remember a single sermon where he preached on the Love of God. This is how I perceived and understood my father's teaching of the Gospel.

His preaching and beliefs were filled with a lot of things you "couldn't do"; never anything that you "could do" as a Christian. I was not allowed to wear pants, nail polish or any type of make-up growing up as his child. I couldn't go to the movies or spend the night with my friends. I wasn't allowed to listen to any type of music other than Gospel. I was not allowed to watch Soul Train or any secular shows on television as a child either; but of course every chance I got, I would sneak and watch it anyway.

He would make all of us "fast" with him. I was told not to eat breakfast at school. I think I may have been in the 3rd grade when I remember going to school one day and having to just sit at the table and not eat my breakfast. I was afraid of my father and the discipline

29

that I would receive if I disobeyed him. Not only did he put the fear of God in me, I feared him as well. My dad would give me this certain look that made me literally feel as though he had whipped me with his eyes.

He taught me that once I reached or passed the age of 12, I was going to be held accountable for every sin that I committed. I believe he may have come to this conclusion because of the age of Jesus in the Bible when he was talking to the doctors in Jerusalem. (Luke 2:42-52)

When I was around 12 years old, I mentioned to my dad that I thought about drowning myself in the bathtub. His response to me was very cold; he said "If you do, in hell you will lift up your eyes." I knew I didn't want to go to hell, so I never thought about drowning myself again.

While typing this, in my mind, I am asking questions again. "What made my father be the man he was?" "Why did he only teach us about the wrath of God, instead of God's love for us?" "Where did he get his understanding of the WORD? "Why, when I told him about my thoughts of drowning, did he not ask me my reasoning for wanting to do that? "Why did every bad thing I did after age 12 have to send me to hell?"

CHAPTER 3
THE SECOND DEATH

In January 1976, my step-mother gave birth to a baby girl. I can't quite remember the pregnancy at all; I just remember seeing the baby.

Almost seven months later, on a Friday night, August 13, 1976, my baby brother passed away at two and a half years of age. He was what some would say, 30 months old. I recently obtained a copy of his death certificate to confirm what caused his death and it lists pneumonia. Please allow me to tell you what I remember happening. This didn't come from what anyone told me, this is what I saw with my own eyes and I do not believe it was a dream; it was too real.

Earlier on the morning of my brother's death, my step-mother had cooked some grits for us to eat. My baby brother ate all of his and asked for some more. My step-mother took his plate, which looked to me to be an old round cake pan, and put some more grits in it. It was enough grits to cover the entire bottom of the pan. My brother began to eat it, but he couldn't finish all of it. This seemed to make my step-mother angry, or so I thought. She began to fuss at him and tell him to eat the grits. He couldn't. The next thing I remember is her taking my baby brother to the bathroom. She took with her a red cup filled with water and a switch. **(To those of you who don't know what a switch is, it is a small branch broken off of a tree. The leaves are taken off, and then you get a whipping with it.)** Anyway, she started whipping my brother and pouring water on his head at the same time. He was fully clothed at the time. I know this may sound crazy or absurd to you, but I am telling you what I saw. I stood in the hallway and watched her do this to him. This is truly what is stored in my memory to this day. My baby brother was just-a-crying his little heart out. I stood there, a helpless six-year old child, and couldn't do a thing to save my little brother, "*my baby*." I see it just as if it happened yesterday. I can even see myself taking the left over grits from his plate and throwing it out to the dog.

After she was done whipping him, I don't remember my baby brother walking again. He may have, I just don't remember it.

Later that afternoon, she loaded all of us children in her car and we all went to clean the church for services that night. I couldn't help clean up because I had to take care of my little brother. I sat outside on the porch of the church and laid my baby brother's head in my lap. I just rubbed his little head; that's all I remember doing for him.

Later that evening, when my dad came home from work, I went into the bedroom where he was. My baby brother was lying in the baby bed. He was lying there still, not even giving a reaction to mine or my daddy's presence. I couldn't tell if he was awake or asleep, but I felt that my dad knew something was wrong with him. The family loaded up into two separate cars, my siblings and I with daddy and my step-siblings with their mom and we headed to church. That was the norm; we never went to our church in one car as a family. There was always a separation.

On the way to church, my dad stopped by a Seven Eleven store and purchased a small jar of apple juice. He gave it to my baby brother to drink. My brother may have taken two sips of it and that was all. We went on to church, once we got inside, somebody took my baby brother to the very back of the church and laid him down. Daddy was in the pulpit praying, my step-mother and her sister were in the back of the church where my brother was and they were praying for him, I guess. This seemed to go on for hours. They prayed and prayed and prayed. After a while, as I was looking back there (my siblings and I were sitting in front of the church) at my step-mother and her sister, my baby brother sat up. It seemed as if he looked directly at me. He stared and then he lay back down. (I now know that he was saying good-bye to me)

Soon after I witnessed my brother lay back down, the door of the church opened up and in walked my grandmother and a close friend of hers. My grandmother asked where my baby brother was and went towards the back of the church. It was as if she knew something had happened or was happening to him. When she looked at my brother, she told my daddy that he needed to take him to the hospital right then. My daddy picked my baby brother up and carried him out of the church. As he passed by me, I could see white spit coming out the side of my baby brother's mouth.

When we got to the hospital, my dad carried my baby brother into the emergency room. My grandmother, her friend and I followed him inside but stayed in the waiting room. My step-mother stayed outside in her car with her children. My baby brother was pronounced DOA (dead on arrival) at 11:45 pm.

About a week or so prior to my baby brother's death, we were visiting our grandparents' home. My brother climbed up on the piano stool and reached on top of the piano and opened up a bottle of my grandfather's heart medicine. He put a handful of the red pills in his mouth. I happened to glance at him and noticed what he had done. I called for grandma to come help me get the pills out of my baby brother's mouth. She came running in the room where we were and proceeded to make him spit the pills out. To this day, my dad and step-mother believed that was the cause of my brother's death. (My grandmother did consult my grandfather's doctor about the incident and the doctor told her that the pills would not have hurt my little brother. He said that if anything, they would have helped him.)

Now I am no doctor, but in my opinion, I believe that if my brother had truly swallowed any of my grandfather's medicine, he would have had an immediate reaction to it. However, he did not, so I beg to differ with my parents' belief of his cause of death. Surely it wouldn't have taken days or possibly a week or two later for the medicine to cause my brother to die.

Nevertheless, only God knows why this happened to my baby brother. God knew what was best. As a songwriter once said, ***"God will never put more on you than you can bear."*** God in His infinite wisdom knew that I couldn't raise my baby brother and my sisters along with what was coming ahead in my life. I believe God took my baby brother on home with Him to free me up to further fulfill the destiny He had planned for my life.

As I am writing this, I am asking myself why my dad didn't take my brother to the hospital or even ask my step-mother what happened to him... I had to take a break from writing, get up, go outside and have a good cry. As an adult, I know that I have NEVER cried or grieved over the death of my brother. Who knew this day, June 26, 2011; I would become overwhelmed with grief and cry the way I cried today. (When I picked up my netbook to work on and edit my book tonight, May 9, 2012... I cried and grieved again) I am sure I cried as a child, but that is not a part of my memory. But today, I thank God for the good cry I just experienced. I never knew that I was still carrying that hurt inside of me for my baby brother; my baby.... Another part of my complete healing! Thank YOU Jesus!

CHAPTER 4
Molestation and Raping

Sometime later, I'm guessing I was seven or eight years old, the enemy used my oldest step-brother who was around 12 or 13 at the time, to completely take away and destroy my childhood innocence. Yes, my oldest step-brother began to molest and rape me every opportunity he got. Every time my dad and step-mother left the house, my step-brother used that time to rape and molest me. He would call me back to his bedroom and close the door and do his thing. This would go on for the next five or six years of my life. He made me do things to and for him that would make your stomach turn.

The first time he raped me, I experienced the most excruciating pain I had ever felt in my entire life. He was not gentle at all. I really didn't know what was happening to me, all I knew was it hurt. He would ejaculate on me and tell me to go bathe in a hurry because I could get pregnant. He threatened to beat me up if I told anyone about what he was doing to me. I was terrified of him; I really believed he would beat me up real bad if I told.

During all of the molestation and rape, I would cry and cry. It did not phase my step-brother at all. Although he had several girlfriends throughout his high school years, he kept on using me for his pleasure time after time after time. This would go on up until after he graduated from high school. My youngest step-brother molested me as well. He never raped me, but would get naked, lie on top of me and hunch and fondle me. No matter what happened or which one did it, molestation is molestation.

At around age 13, during the Thanksgiving Holidays from school, I started my period. My step-mother knew about it. A few days later, I went into the bathroom and began shampooing my hair. My step-mother made the comment to me, "You're in there washing your hair, you are going to be dead somewhere." My step-brother overheard my step-mother talking to me and asked her why she was telling me that. She went on to tell him that I had started my period. From that day to this one, neither of my step-brothers ever raped or molested me again.

There again, God was working in my life. He knew if my step-brother kept on raping me, I could have gotten pregnant and I couldn't bear that. God knew the exact timing for the raping and molestation to cease. Here again was a very traumatic experience for me, but I had to go through it so my sisters wouldn't have to. I was their protector, I believe that.

Sometime after that, I believe I was around 14 years of age; my dad came in the mobile home and starting having a conversation with me and my two sisters. I don't remember the exact content of what we were talking about, but my dad asked me if I was a virgin. I bluntly told him no. I don't remember his reaction to my answer. I then began to tell him about the raping and the molestation that happened to me years earlier. (My oldest step-brother had gotten married by this time and my youngest step-brother was off in college) I could hardly believe my dad's response to what I had just shared with him. He said to me, "I figured that was going on." Those were his exact words to me! Wow! What a blow to my little heart! I'm thinking in my mind, "If you figured it was going on, then why didn't you do something about it?" I was at a complete loss for words at that moment. Then I asked my dad why he didn't ask me about it. He answered me by saying that he had asked my step-brother about it and he denied it was going on. He then asked me why didn't I come to him and tell him about it. I explained to him that I was terrified of my step-brother and that he threatened to beat me up if I told on him.

My dad left the mobile home and went into the house to inform my step-mother of what he had just found out from me. Because our bedroom window was right outside of the house's kitchen window and they both were open, I could hear my dad and step-mother talking. My step-mother's response to my dad was and I quote, "She probably asked for it." I could not believe my ears!

"How could I have asked for something I knew nothing about?" I asked myself in disbelief. I immediately started crying. My dad came back into the mobile home and hugged me. I don't remember

39

him saying, at that time, that he was sorry for what had happened to me. However, he did make certain to explain to me, "***Whatever happened in the house, stayed in the house.***"

How could my dad have been so dense? How could he have continued to allow me to suffer because of a choice that he selfishly made years before? Why didn't he protect me? Why didn't he take legal action against my step-brother right then and there? Why did he choose to keep the raping and molestation a secret? Why did he choose to protect a man who was not his biological son instead of protecting me, his own flesh and blood? Did he not love me? Did he not believe me?

A few days after that, I asked my dad if I could go and visit my grandmother. He told me to go ask my step-mother. When I asked her, she said to me, "No, you can't go over there!" "All y'all want to do is go over there and be a bunch of whores!"

In my mind, I wanted to say to her, "If I am a whore, your son made me one."

In May of 1993, I got the opportunity to confront both of my step-brothers one-on-one about the raping and molestation. I went to my youngest step-brother first. As I was talking to him, tears came to his eyes. He then told me that he had just been thinking on the very same thing. He immediately apologized for what he had done to me. We hugged each other and I told him that I loved him like a brother.

When I approached my oldest step-brother, he first said that we were both just children when the raping and molestation happened. He quickly denied remembering any of it. I wanted an apology out of him so badly, that I looked him directly in his eyes and apologized to him three different times; desperately hoping for an apology. I know I didn't owe him an apology, but I was giving him the opportunity to apologize to me. I even told him that I was sorry if I did anything or looked at him any kind of way for him to approach me. I felt in my heart, that if he would apologize to me, all the hurt and pain would go away.

I left his presence feeling a loss. I was hurt and wondered why he wouldn't admit to what he did to me. Why did he choose me? What did I do to make him hate me so badly? He never apologized, and hasn't to this day.

CHAPTER 5
EVER BEEN HUNGRY?

During the summers after both my step-brothers had moved out, my step-mother would leave food for my step-sisters and my half-sisters to eat. She would put the food in my step-sisters bedroom, so that my sisters and I wouldn't have access to it. She didn't leave us anything; so we had to pretty much fend for ourselves during the day. Sometimes, I would go in the bedroom while my step-sisters were asleep and steal some of the food and take it back to the mobile home to share it with my sisters. Plenty of times, my sisters and I would plot to steal milk, cereal, and sugar out of the house. We would decide who would take what, even down to the spoon and the bowl. In my opinion, no child should ever have to steal food.

See, when my oldest step-brother was still living at home, he made it known to me and my sisters that all the food in house belonged to their family. It was not ours. Our parents would buy breakfast cereal and milk for the children to eat. However, only my step-siblings were allowed to eat it. I mentioned in an earlier chapter how we went to church hungry on Sunday mornings; well this is why. If my sisters and I ate any cereal, we had to steal it. You have to understand, as I have said before, we were terrified of our oldest step-brother. To me, he was my boss. I was more afraid of him than I was of my dad; and I was sorely afraid of my dad. Whenever my step-brother asked me or my sisters a question, we had to respond to him with a "yes sir" or a "no sir." That was the way he instructed us to answer him.

Years later, after I got the chance to tell my dad about the cereal incidents, my step-mother accused me of lying about her. She stated that the food was left for my half-sisters because they were younger. She also said she had no knowledge of us not being able to eat the cereal on Sunday mornings and that we could have eaten it if we wanted to. But through it all, God was still in control.

One summer, I believe I may have been 15 years old; some apartment buildings were being built behind our house. Every day after the workers would leave for the day; my sisters and I would go to the apartment buildings and scavenge for leftovers. We would find half-eaten sandwiches, opened bags of potato chips, opened bottles of soda pops, etc. Thank God for who's ever idea it was to build those apartments behind our house!

One particular day, when my middle sister and I were outside playing, a dog ran past us. I noticed the dog was carrying a piece of aluminum foil in his mouth. I said to my sister, "Girl, he's got some food in his mouth!" I took off running behind the dog hoping he would drop whatever he had in his mouth. I didn't care what it was, I just had a feeling it was food. Sure enough the dog dropped it. I picked it up and opened it to discover it was a red-hot link sausage wrapped in a slice of light bread. I broke it in half and shared it with my sister.

My mind goes back to the prophet Elijah, when God told him to go hide himself and He would send the ravens to feed him. (1 Kings 17:1-6) God was feeding my sisters and me that summer, from His own hands.

I have since had the opportunity to share the story about the dog with my dad. He said he had no idea that we were hungry. I suppose he assumed we were okay, because he never asked us. I don't know why my dad wasn't aware of what was going on with us. That's another question that has never been answered.

My sisters and I spent a lot of time playing during the summer. We truly enjoyed and loved each other. We played all sorts of imaginary games to escape the "real" world. I would pretend to be their school teacher and they would be my students. I would teach them reading, spelling, math and my favorite was music. They really seemed to enjoy it and I loved it as well. Oftentimes, we would pretend that we were a family doing a television show that we made up. I would play the role of the "mom" and again they were my children. We would ride our bicycles up and down the dirt road for hours on end. Sometimes my other "sisters' would join us outside and play hide and seek, kick ball, leap frog, hop scotch, and many other childhood games.

Most every summer afternoon when my dad came home from work, he would go fishing. I went with him on many occasions. I can remember quietly sitting there beside my dad on the bank of the river waiting intently for him to catch a fish. My father was quite the fisherman. He would catch a mess often. When he did, my sisters and I would have to clean them. We were the only ones who cleaned fish. We would go outside to the front of the mobile home to clean the fish, and we'd sing, sing and sing. To us, cleaning the fish was very nasty, but the singing took our minds off of it. That is how our "singing group" came to be. Needless to say, even though we were the only ones to clean the fish, we certainly were not the only ones to eat them once they were cooked.

On another note, for some reason, my dad did not whip my step-sisters. I don't know to this day what his reasoning was. However, he did whip both my step-brothers if they did something wrong. My step-mother would whip me and my sisters. It didn't matter what we did, big or small, she would whip us. When we were little, she would take us to her room, make us get down on our knees and lay our heads on her bed as if we were about to pray. She would then sit on our heads and whip us. She said the reason why she did that was so that we could not run away from her while she was whipping us. When we became teenagers, she didn't attempt to sit on our heads anymore. She just whipped us as best as she could, with either a leather belt, or the biggest switch she could find. After a while, the whippings stopped hurting us.

(Earlier today, August 19, 2012, as I was once again editing my book, my daughter and I were in Wal-Mart shopping for groceries. As I was looking for some sausage and bacon, I saw a package of "Red Hots" and immediately my mind went back to the day when I took that one from the dog. From that day until this one, I have never eaten another Red Hot again.)

CHAPTER 6
"GET OUT OF MY HOUSE!"

Toward the end of the summer of 1985, there seemed to be complete turmoil in the house between my sisters and our two step-sisters. They began to physically fight, several times a day, every day. There was no question, we disliked each other. I don't think it was anything that was planned; it just kind of ended up that way. My sisters and I were never accepted as part of the family. When we were isolated in the mobile home away from them, the separation began and never ended. There was a lot of hostility and animosity going on between the children. The hate had grown so thick you could have cut it with a knife.

I remember the time when my step-sister's light bulb had blown in her bedroom. I heard my step-mother in the room saying, "Dianna probably stole your light bulb; I bet you their light bulb blew and she came in here and changed it." After a while, my baby half-sister, who was about eight or nine at the time, came in the kitchen where I was and repeated what my step-mother said. I denied it and attempted to ignore her. My step-mother came in the kitchen fussing and told my baby half-sister to get in my face and say it. I got up and attempted to go out to the mobile home. My step-mother stepped in front of me to stop me. So, I pushed up against her with my body trying to get her to let me out. She really got mad then and accused me of trying to fight her, which I was not. She was yelling it out so that my dad could hear her. She said if I was trying to fight her, it was time for me to go. That was her way of telling me to get out of her house. She got a belt and proceeded to whip me for that incident; one that she caused and I tried to avoid. Ephesians 6:4 says, *"And, ye fathers, provoke not your children to wrath: but bring them up in the nurture and admonition of the LORD."* My dad did nothing that I know of, about the fight that my step-mother tried to start.

Later that week, my youngest step-sister and I got into a fight in the mobile home. She started an argument with me for no apparent reason. My dad happened to be in the mobile home at the time. He never said a word to me or my step-sister. As we fought, I had gotten her down on the bed and was beating the daylights out of her. Somehow, my step-mother found out we were fighting and out to the mobile home she came. She started hitting me on my back with her fist and telling me to leave her daughter alone. By this time, my dad intervened; broke everything up and stood between me and my step-mother. My step-mother yelled at me, "I want you gone! Get out of my house!"

I yelled back to her, "This is my trailer!" The reason I said this to her is because a while before, my dad had told me the mobile home was mine.

She yelled back, "Well, if your name is on this trailer, I want it off my land and on the road! I mean it; if you want to beat on somebody, have your own child!" She stormed out of the mobile home and my dad followed right behind her never saying a word.

The next morning before my step-mother left for work, she came into my bedroom and spoke directly to me, "If you are not out of my house when I get home today, I will have the police get you out!"

Shortly after she left the house, my dad came in my bedroom and said, "You all just go up town and stay there all day until I get home." Up town was the city part of the small town we lived in. It was the area where the post office, grocery store, gas station, bank and the pharmacy were located. It was about a mile from where our house was located.

I don't know what my dad was thinking or what may have been his reasoning for telling us to go up town and stay all day. He didn't give a precise destination, just "up town". In my opinion, he didn't take his role as a man in the house that day. I'm not sure what the problem was or why he didn't step up to his wife and take complete control over the situation. Secretly, deep down inside of him, it would have been and was a relief to him for us to leave. I know that because he later told me so out of his own mouth. He stated to me that he was trying to keep peace.

After my dad left for work, my middle sister and I decided that we would leave. We had no intentions on coming back home. My youngest sister wanted to follow us, but I told her to stay because she was too young. I believe she was 12 years old at the time. Plus I figured if she went, my dad would surely make us come back home. My middle sister and I walked up town and went straight to my grandmother's job. We told her what happened and what our dad had instructed us to do. She then gave me a key to her house and instructed us to go there and we could live with her. (My grandfather had passed away years earlier)

Thank God for continuing to watch over us. He had already provided a home for my sister and me. Isn't that just like God? He had it all in control.

It's a good thing that we left home when we did. My sisters and I had secretly planned to burn my step-mother's house down with her in it. We planned to use some of the gasoline that was used for the lawn mower to start the fire. I look back now and think how the plan would have never worked, but in our minds we had hoped it would.

About six months later, my youngest sister came to live with us at our grandmother's house. We never lived with our dad again.

My dad did attempt several times to talk us into coming back home, but he didn't try very hard. I think he may have done it out of obligation, not because he truly wanted us to come back home. He realized that living with our grandmother was the best thing, not only for us, but for him as well. Now, he wouldn't have to feel like he was "in the middle" anymore, which he really wasn't; he was on my step-mother's side all the time.

CHAPTER 7
FREE

Life was wonderful for me. My childhood was long gone, but I felt free as a bird. I was back at home with "my mom". I no longer had the responsibility of taking care of my sisters. I, we had a caregiver again! I could finally live my life for me.

My grandmother showered us with warmth and love. She encouraged us to love each other and not fuss and fight with one another. She reminded us, my sisters and I, that we were all we had. I am reminded of the scripture Ecclesiastes 4:12, "*And if one prevail against him, two shall withstand him; and a threefold cord is not easily broken.*" Truly, I can say today, that my sisters and I are a "threefold cord."

We had constant contact with my dad. He would come over and bring my grandmother groceries from time to time. He would also pick us up for his weekly church services. Eventually he stopped bringing my grandmother groceries and started giving her $20 a week. My grandmother graciously accepted it and I never, not once, heard her complain about it.

Back in 1985 $20 was worth more than it is now in 2011. Naturally, $20 wouldn't have been enough money to support my sisters and me, but God made the money stretch. My grandmother always had plenty of food for us and anyone else who came by and wanted to eat. I never went hungry again. I never had to steal food again. I had a warm bed to sleep in at night. I felt like I was in heaven. In a sense, I was. God had snatched me from the hands of the enemy. I thank Him for the much needed relief. However, there were many more trials awaiting me in the coming years.

At age 16, my junior year in high school, I became a basketball cheerleader. What an exciting time in my life! As I stated before, while living at home with my dad, he didn't allow us to wear pants or fingernail polish. We couldn't go to the ball games or to the movies. So, I was ecstatic to finally be able to do these things.

Being a basketball cheerleader gave me the opportunity to visit places I had never gone before. I loved it. I began to meet people, especially boys. I can't begin to explain the new-found joy and peace I was experiencing for the first time in my life.

During that time, I became sexually active with a guy I had a crush on. He never acknowledged me as his girlfriend in public. I guess it was because he was what some would call a "ladies man" and due to the fact that he had a "main" girlfriend.

Even though this guy never acknowledged me as his girlfriend, it was no secret that we liked each other. As long as I got my time with him, I didn't care about being number one in his life. Little did I know at the time, I was selling myself short. This guy never took me out on a "real" date. He never took me out to eat nor to the movies. This became my tradition with other guys as well. For the next few years of my life, I was second choice to other guys, never number one.

In February 1987, at age 17, I graduated early from high school. I and the guy had stopped seeing each other and I felt I needed to get out of town for a vacation. I was in love with him, but he didn't feel the same way about me.

I decided to go to Florida to visit my great-aunt. While down there, my cousin introduced me to his cousin. This guy and I began to date; we quickly hit it off. He was a pretty nice guy. He took me out to eat and to the movies. I had not experienced this with any other guy. I began to really like him a lot. After about three months of dating him, we had sex and I got pregnant with my oldest son. I knew that I was pregnant before I left Florida because I missed my monthly right after the first sexual encounter with him. I can remember praying and begging God to please let it come on. I mean, I lay across my bed and begged and begged and begged. After I got through crying, it was as if the Holy Spirit led me to pick up my aunt's Bible. I opened it up and the pages fell on James, Chapter 4. I kid you not! So, I started reading the chapter. When I got to verse 3, my mouth fell open. Never in my life do I remember reading that before. It read, *"Ye ask, and receive not because ye ask amiss, that ye may consume it upon your lusts."* I then picked up the dictionary and looked up the word "amiss." I found out that it meant "in a wrong way". I then knew in my heart that God was not going to answer my prayer.

At the end of May, I had to leave Florida because I had to go back home to graduate the following June. I left without telling the guy that I was pregnant. I didn't know what I was going to tell my family. I had gotten pregnant by a guy I hardly knew. I wondered what people would think of me now.

When I got back to my grandmother's house, I didn't tell her I was pregnant because I was too ashamed of what I had done. Somehow, she knew. She looked at me one day directly in my eyes and asked me if I was pregnant. I admitted to her that I was, and asked her how she knew. She went on to explain to me about my neck looking a certain way and she could tell by that. She didn't scold me or talk down to me about my pregnancy. I could tell she was a little disappointed, but she never said it. She did remind me that I would have to take care of my own baby.

Telling my dad about my pregnancy was a totally different story. I wanted him to hear it from me instead of hearing about it in the streets. I went to visit him at his home one evening. Before I could even say anything to him, he told me that he heard that I was pregnant and asked me if it was true. I told him yes. The very next words that came out of his mouth still linger in my ears to this very day. His blunt response to me was, "That which has been done is deadly." He walked out and left me standing in the kitchen, alone. He didn't hug me, tell me he loved me or even assure me that everything would be alright; nothing. I can't even begin to explain how those words made me feel at that very moment. I thought I was the worst daughter in the world. All I ever wanted was my dad to love me. I felt like a knife had pierced my heart.

My interpretation of what my dad had just told me was that I was going straight to hell because I had gotten pregnant! I now know that was a very untrue statement, but he left me believing that lie! How could he condemn me for what I had done, but never condemn my step-brothers for the raping and molestation? Were they going to hell for what they did to me? I left my dad's house feeling devastated and alone. I had let my dad down…

I felt like running far away and far away wasn't nearly far enough. I was already ashamed of the fact of getting pregnant without being married. Now on top of that, I was going to hell for it. One thing for sure, I was going to have my baby and take care of it.

I didn't want people to know that I went to Florida and got pregnant, so I came up with a plan to somehow justify my pregnancy. I contacted the guy that I dated back before I went to Florida. I had sex with him so that I could tell him later on that I was pregnant. My plan worked. When I told him about my being pregnant, he wanted me to have an abortion. In fact, he offered to take me to Savannah, GA, to have the procedure done. I told him absolutely not. I was keeping my baby.

A few weeks after my graduation, my grandmother helped me get a job at a hospital, but after about three months, I decided to leave Georgia and go to Philadelphia to stay with my God-Mother until my baby was born. I became very homesick. I called my grandmother almost every single day, sometimes more than once. She would oftentimes say to me that I should have stayed in Georgia. I would call my father every now and then. I distinctly remember one phone call I had with him, I asked him if I could have the mobile home once I came back home to Georgia with my baby. His response to me was that my step-mother needed somewhere to store her furniture and that possibly her brother would be living in it. As I type this, I sit here shaking my head once again. Where was the love? I don't know.

While I was in Philadelphia; I got the opportunity to meet some of my dad's side of the family. It was my dad's uncle and his wife and children. My great-uncle passed away only a few months after I met him. My dad and some more of my family from Georgia traveled to Philadelphia to attend the funeral. I was so happy to see my family from home. After the funeral was over and they were getting ready to go back home, my dad hugged me and told me that he loved me. I broke down and began to cry. I hugged him harder, as I cried, and didn't want to let him go. I felt so much joy and happiness in my heart. That would be the second time in my life that I remember my dad telling me he loved me.

When I was eight months pregnant, I decided to make a phone call to my son's "biological" father in Florida. I told him I was pregnant and he bluntly told me the child I was carrying was not his and hung-up in my face. He denied his child. I was hurt by his response, but I really couldn't blame him. I left Florida knowing I was pregnant and deliberately hid it from him. And to make matters worse, I had another guy believing it was his child. Nevertheless, I was determined to keep my baby and was prepared to raise him by myself. It would be 12 years before I would talk to my son's biological father again.

February 9, 1988, the morning before my baby's birth, I was at the hospital all alone. I wasn't scared or anything, but I just wanted someone to be with me. I wanted my grandmother with me. After over 26 hours of being in labor, I birthed a healthy 8 lb. 13 oz. baby boy. When I was taken out of the delivery room my God-Mother was waiting on me in the hallway with a big smile on her face.

When my baby was one day short of being a month old, I boarded the train and headed back home to Georgia. I knew I was not going to live off of my grandmother. I was going to take care of myself and my baby. I got my job back at the hospital and in August of 1988, moved into my own apartment. In fact, it was the very same apartment complex that my sisters and I had scavenged food from years earlier. I was 18 years old at this time. My grandmother took it upon herself to raise my baby as her own. She did this for the first two years of his life.

CHAPTER 8
The Little Whore

I appreciated my grandmother for taking my son and raising him for me as her own. I provided for him financially. She didn't have to spend her money on him for anything, unless she wanted to. She helped me out a lot by relieving me of the responsibility of totally caring for him. I never took her for granted. She was always there for me when I needed her. She had such a loving, caring and nurturing heart towards me. I thank God for her. Had He not allowed me to feel love from her, I don't know where I would be right now.

Because my grandmother was taking care of my son, that left room for me to be free once again. I could go out dancing and partying whenever I got ready. I started going out to clubs on a regular basis. I would go out every Wednesday, Thursday, Friday, Saturday and Sunday night to different clubs in different cities. I was enjoying life again. I did not do drugs, smoke nor drink. I just enjoyed dancing and hanging out.

For the next year and a half of my life, I began to meet men and literally became the "whore" my step-mother labeled me as years earlier. Parents, be careful what you call your children. You never know what seed you may be planting in them. I don't ever remember having sex with a man because I loved him or because he claimed to have loved me. I only had sex with him because he wanted to. I was afraid if I didn't have sex with him, he wouldn't like me anymore.

To further complicate matters for me, I would like the man up until I had sex with him, then it was as if I hated him right afterwards. This brings back to my mind the portion of scripture in the Old Testament, 2 Samuel 13 where David's son Am'non was in love with his blood sister, Ta'mar. He loved her until he raped her. Then he hated her more than he ever loved her. That is how I would feel about a guy after I had been with him.

I began to have a bitter taste in my mouth as far as sex was concerned. Still, I continued to do this over and over and over again.

It was like I couldn't say "no". I did not enjoy having sex at all. I never experienced any pleasure with any of the men I had sex with. It became a way of life for me, day after day, week after week, month after month.

After a while, I got tired of the way I was living. I wanted to be loved. I wanted a real relationship. I wanted someone to love me for me and not for what they could get from me. I wanted a steady, meaningful relationship with one man. So I decided in my mind, I was going to quit having sex just to be having sex. I realized, at age 19, that I was better than that and I wanted more for my life.

I had some lonely nights at home, but I didn't wake up the next morning with a man lying next to me that I couldn't stand. I felt a sense of peace. I had taken control of my life once again. I knew I was raised better than that.

CHAPTER 9
Engaged and Married

On October 31, 1989, I began working at a women's pants factory. It was there that I was introduced by my cousin to a cousin of hers, who also worked there. (What was it with my cousins introducing me to people?) The guy and I began to date. He would come by my grandmother's house every evening to see me after we got off work. I would go to my grandmother's house every day to see my son and also to eat her good cooking. She always made sure I had a lunch to take to work every day.

He would visit with me until around 11pm each night and then take me home to my apartment. He never asked to come in. He was a very shy 20 year old man, and quite the gentlemen. He was also very sweet and caring. Most of all, he loved my son. He didn't try to come on to me or get fresh with me at all. He was different from all the other guys I had encountered. I was impressed by his behavior towards me. He would take me out to the movies and take me and my son out to dinner; all without asking for anything in return.

During the Thanksgiving holidays, we were given a few days off from work. I instructed the guy NOT to come visit me during those days because I would be going out every night I was off. He didn't listen to me; he came anyway. It was funny to me that he would come after I had asked him not to.

November 23, 1989, Thanksgiving evening, he and I had just come back from a friends' house. He was getting ready to leave to go home and I was getting ready to go out clubbing. Just before I was about to get out of his car, he said to me, "I want to marry you." I looked at him and laughed. He had not even held my hand or kissed me. In fact, I don't think he had even touched me at all at this point.

"Marry me? You don't even know me." I responded. Although we had been dating, I really didn't consider him my boyfriend. "That don't matter," he answered. "I still want to marry you."

Before I could say anything more, my grandmother came to the front door of the house and informed me that she wasn't keeping my son that night. She wanted me to take him home with me so that she could get some rest. But you know me; I was looking forward to going out. Right at that moment, he offered to take my son home with him that night so that I could go out! I didn't think twice about his offer. I got out of the car, went into the house, packed my son's baby bag, got his car seat and loaded it into his car. I sent my son home with him. I can still see the disapproving look on my grandmother's face, but she never said a word to me.

I look back on that today and think of how immature, selfish and careless that was of me. I was enjoying my life so much; I wouldn't give it up for my own child. I didn't know this young man well enough to allow him to take my child to his home, especially overnight. But God protected my son in spite of my immature decision.

While at the club on the dance floor, I began thinking about the young man and how he took my son with him so that I could go out to party. In my mind I began to think, "Why am I out here at a club, when the kind of man I want is at home with my son?" The thought only lingered briefly. I soon forgot about it and continued to enjoy myself throughout the night.

The next day he brought my son back to my grandmother's house safe and sound.

On Tuesday, December 5, 1989, flowers were delivered to me on my job. It was my 20th birthday. He had sent them to me. Later that evening, as he was taking me home from my grandmother's house, he asked me if I would be his girlfriend. I told him that I would think about it. When we got to my apartment, he asked me, "Can I get a kiss?"

I kind of smiled and responded, "Not in your car." We got out of the car; he followed me to my apartment. He stood just inside the door. He did not sit down and I didn't offer him a seat.

65

"Who lives here with you?" He asked. "Nobody, I live here by myself." I answered, as I placed the flowers on the kitchen table. I then walked over to the door where he was standing. We hugged each other and he kissed me. Oh what a beautiful kiss it was. After the kiss was over, he told me good night, walked out the door and left. I couldn't believe it. I was shocked that this man did not attempt to sleep with me. Deep in my heart I felt this was the type of man I wanted to marry. Needless to say, I accepted the offer of being his girlfriend.

During the Christmas holidays, my boyfriend's mother decided to go out of town to visit her mother. She wanted my boyfriend to go with her, but he refused to go. He was determined to spend the holidays with me. His mother told him that she was locking her house up until she got back, so I offered my boyfriend a place to stay for the week.

The first night at my apartment, he began to make his bed on my couch. I went in the living room where he was and told him that he didn't have to sleep on the couch. I invited him into my bedroom. Without me saying, you know what happened next.

December 25, 1989, Christmas Day, my boyfriend presented me with an engagement ring at my grandmother's house. He got down on his knees and asked me to marry him. I accepted. We became officially engaged.

After the Christmas holidays were over, my fiancé was supposed to go back home to stay; that never happened. He moved into my apartment with me. I never wanted my grandmother to find out that I was shacking up. She never asked me about it and I never told her. If she knew, she never confronted me or asked me about it.

May 5, 1990, we were married. My husband suggested that I needed to take my two-year-old son from my grandmother and raise him myself. I agreed with him.

My grandmother didn't argue or persuade me to leave my son with her. I never once asked her how she felt about me taking my son from her. I never even considered her feelings. I wonder if she had the same feelings she had when my dad took me from her years earlier. I will never know.

Looking back, I see the huge mistake I made in shacking up with my boyfriend. I should have never let him move in with me or invited him into my bedroom. I should have waited on God. I didn't do that. I let my flesh make the decision for me. I didn't have the mind to wait on God at that time. I felt very guilty about shacking up, but I didn't want my boyfriend to move out. I married out of fleshly reasons, because I knew shacking up was wrong. I now feel that had I not shacked up, my life may have turned out very different than it has.

CHAPTER 10
CONFESSIONS

Shortly after my husband and I were married, he lost his job. He was unemployed for the next fifteen months of our marriage. Financially this was a tough time for us as newlyweds. I began to feel like I had two children instead of one. During the time that he was unemployed; he lost his driver's license due to an unpaid traffic ticket for having the windows on his car tinted too dark. I began to resent my husband for the pressure he was putting on me. Not only did he not have a job, now he could not look for one.

Sex, for me, wasn't good at all. As I stated earlier, I had never had a pleasurable sexual experience, but I knew there had to be more to sex than what I was feeling. I was a pro at faking and my husband had no idea.

I had told my husband about the raping and the molestation, but not about my promiscuous lifestyle before I met him. One day, I decided to let him in on my past sex life. I sat down and wrote down every name; yes I knew the name of every guy I had sex with. I gave the list to my husband. I then confessed to him that I had been faking all my life and with him also. He was flabbergasted, to say the least. He became very angry at me and accused me of lying to him and tricking him into marrying me. He went on to say that he thought I was different from all the other girls.

My loving husband turned into this evil man. He started to physically abuse me. We would get into an argument and he would punch me with his fist to make me shut my mouth. He would curse me out and call me all kinds of names. Of course, he would apologize and assure me that he wouldn't do it again. But, as you may have guessed, it became the norm for the next couple of years of my life. I truly feel in my heart that my husband began to secretly hate me. After that, sex was really just sex. It was as if he didn't care about me at all. It became my duty as a wife to perform, nothing more. He would do his thing and get up, never asking me how I felt or if there was anything he could do to help me enjoy sex. I felt like that little whore all over again, except this time, it was with my husband.

During this time, there would be many break-ups and getting back together with my husband. I would leave and go stay with my grandmother for weeks at a time; then he would convince me to come back home. This would happen numerous times over the course of the next year.

My advice to you reader, let your past stay in your past. As long as it is not going to cause you or your mate any physical harm, let sleeping dogs lie. I don't know what possessed me to tell my husband about my past. The only thing I really wanted to get over to him was that I was not enjoying sex and that I felt as though I was missing out on something. I was tired of doing that and wanted more out of our supposedly "making love" boring routine. I didn't know how to communicate that with my husband without bringing up my past.

CHAPTER 11
OUR BABY, HIS AFFAIR

Eventually, my husband would get his license re-instated and find a job. He began to work the midnight shift. Six months later, I got pregnant with my youngest son. I remember the day very well when I went to the health department for my annual pap smear.

My husband had taken me to the health department, but stayed in the waiting room while I was taken to the examination room. Once inside, I told the nurse that my period was two days late. She advised me to take a pregnancy test before going any further with my examination. The test was positive. At that very moment, I was very happy. I asked the nurse not to tell my husband; I wanted to tell him myself. I could hardly wait to share the good news with him.

As my husband and I walked out of the health department to the car, I eagerly and happily told him that I was pregnant. The next words that came out of my mind were devastating. He said to me, "You got pregnant at the wrong time." I could have passed out.

"Wrong time?" I asked, "How could this be the wrong time? You were the one who has been begging me for months to get pregnant!" I exclaimed. "You said that if I had a baby from you our marriage would be better!" His response to me was a simple, "It just is."

I was hurt. Here I was pregnant again and the man didn't want the baby. "How could this be happening to me with a man who supposedly loves me?" I thought to myself. A few months later, my husband and I got into a heated argument. During the argument, he furiously told me that he wished that I was one of his previous girlfriends and that she was the one pregnant from him instead of me. Hearing those words coming out of his mouth brought tears to my eyes. My heart felt as if someone was twisting it like you would a bath cloth to wring the water out of it.

By the time I was six months pregnant, my husband started coming home later and later in the morning from his job. When I questioned him about it, he explained that he was working overtime. On his regular two days off, he told me he was going to spend one day with "the fellas" and one day with me. Although I was reluctant about the agreement, I accepted it.

On one of my husband's nights of "hanging with the fellas," I awoke about 4:00 in the morning. I felt in my spirit that something was just not right. I felt a strange feeling as if something was leaving my body. I got up out of bed and started pacing the floor. I couldn't call my husband to see where he was; we didn't have cell phones back then. I called my dad from my house phone and explained to him the feeling I was experiencing. He prayed for me and told me to sleep in peace and not to worry about where my husband was.

A couple of weeks later, my husband and I were having a conversation. He began to inform me that my sister's boyfriend was cheating on her. At that time, my husband and my sister's boyfriend worked for the same company, but on different shifts. My husband told me who the girl was and everything. When I got to work the next day, I told my sister everything my husband had told me about her boyfriend.

Later in the week, I went to visit my sister at her house. She was not home, but her boyfriend was. I went on in the house to wait for my sister to come home. Her boyfriend told me that he had something to tell me. He said to me, "Since your husband told on me, I'm gonna tell on him." "What are you talking about?" I asked.

"You know what he told you about me cheating on your sister? Well, he has been doing the very same thing to you," he replied. "He and I both have been going with two sisters. In fact, he's been cheating on you every since he started working. They both work the same shift and when they get off work, he takes her home every morning."

"Are you serious?" I asked. "You mean to tell me that he's been cheating on me for over a year?" I asked, with tears in my eyes. "I knew something was up with him coming home later in the mornings and hanging out with the so-called fellas on his day off."

My sister's boyfriend began to tell me everything he knew about the woman my husband was cheating with. He told me her name, her age, the town she lived in, the color house she lived in, and everything. I left my sister's house speechless and hurt. I went straight home and confronted my husband with the knowledge I obtained. He flatly denied everything. He then suggested that my sister's boyfriend was lying and that he was probably mad because he told on him. I took my husband's word and didn't talk to my sister's boyfriend for a long time after that.

During the rest of my pregnancy, the verbal, mental and physical abuse continued. I stayed on antibiotics because I kept getting vaginal infections and didn't know where they were coming from. My husband would come home after drinking, start an argument with me, physically fight me and then leave the house. This became a regular routine. I felt like I was at my wit's end. I had no one to turn to, but my LORD and Savior, Jesus Christ. I went to church, kneeled at the altar and I received Him as LORD of my life during my pregnancy. That was the best decision I could have ever made in my life.

November 22, 1992, my due date, my husband and I were having one of our arguments. He started fighting with me. As we were fighting, I felt a leakage; I knew at once that my water was leaking. I didn't say a word to my husband. I grabbed my already packed overnight bag and left to go down to my grandmother's house. Once I got there, my water bag completely broke. I didn't bother to call my husband because I was mad at him. He had to go to work that night as well.

About 3am, I called my dad and told him that my water had broken and I needed a ride to the hospital. He came to my grandmother's, picked me up and took me to the hospital. Later that morning around 7am, I called one of my cousins and asked if he would call my husband's job and let him know that I was in the hospital.

My husband made it to the hospital about 9am. He sat at my bedside the entire duration of my labor. At one point, he said to me, "Want me to tell you something that will make you mad?" I think he may have said that in an attempt to make me deliver. "No!" I snapped back, "Because it may be true!"

I delivered an 8 pound 3 ounce baby boy that afternoon, November 23, 1992. (exactly three years from the day my husband first told me that he wanted to marry me)

Upon my release from the hospital, I went home. Every day my grandmother would come to my house after she got off work, to clean up and cook supper for my husband, my oldest son and me. I was so thankful and appreciative of her for doing that for me. She would even do our laundry. God really used her to bless me during that time in my life as He had done so many times before.

About a week after my delivery, we got into an argument. During the argument I turned my back to him to leave the room and he hit my back with his fist. I was stunned! I was shocked that this man would hit me knowing that I was still recovering from giving birth. I mean, I was still bleeding and my body was not ready for the abuse he was about to give me. My oldest son, who was four years old at the time, just stood there and watched with fear in his eyes at what was going on.

I immediately packed my bags, grabbed my baby and my oldest son and left to go stay with my grandmother. I stayed with her for the next three months. My husband would come and visit me and the children every day, but he would go back home to stay.

Christmas of the same year, he told me that he was going Christmas shopping for the kids. I asked him if I could go with him. He told me, "No, I want to do this by myself." I accepted his response, although I was a bit surprised by it.

For Christmas, he purchased several outfits of clothing for the baby and a couple of other toys for our oldest son. Again, I was surprised and pleased that he could go shopping alone and pick out pretty decent things.

In January, 1993, my baby was hospitalized for sleep apnea. He would stop breathing in his sleep. That was a scary time for me and my baby. He ended up having to wear an apnea monitor for about four months after that. I had many sleepless nights during that time. He was a very sickly baby. It seemed as if we lived in the doctor's office for the first two years of his life.

In February, right before I was to return to work from maternity leave, I moved back home with my husband. I knew once I got ready to go back to work, it would be difficult for me to find a babysitter that I could trust. It had to be someone who would be patient enough to take care of my baby's needs. By the Grace of God, I did. For the next three months, I had a wonderful babysitter. She took care of my baby like he was her own. She was a true Godsend.

In May, my husband and I had a falling out again. As I had done many times before, I insisted that he leave. He went to stay with his dad.

On Monday, May 24, 1993, I went to take my baby to the babysitter's house and she wasn't home. I went back home to call her on the phone, but she didn't answer. My grandmother had already gone to her housekeeping job by that time. I went to my job with my baby and explained to my supervisor what happened.

After I left my job, I called my father-in-law's house to see if my husband was there. I wanted to inform him of the situation with the baby-sitter. My father-in-law informed me that my husband was not there and in fact, my husband had not even stayed there the night before.

Immediately I thought in my mind, "I'm going to the town my brother-in-law told me about. I'm going to see if he was telling the truth after all." I had never been to the town before, but had seen road signs telling how to get there. I put my 6-month-old baby in the car and off to the town I went.

Once I got to there, I decided that I was going to ride down every street looking for my husband's car. I came to a red light and saw a young man on a bicycle and asked him if he knew the young lady. The man told me exactly how to get to her house. As soon as I made the turn onto the road to the lady's house, I saw my husband's car parked in front of the house with the hood up. Right beside the car stood my husband and the woman. They looked as if they were about to kiss! I sped my car up, put it in park, jumped out and ran up to my husband and cursed at him. The woman had gone into the house by this time. Once I got close enough to my husband, I attempted to slap him. He backed away before my hand hit his face. So I turned around to go get the woman. Now she was standing on the porch with her mom and sister watching me and my husband. When I proceeded toward the house, my husband grabbed my shirt by the neck and pulled me back. I turned around and hit him in his chest as hard as I could. I was in awe that he did not hit me back!

I thought to myself, "Wait a minute, he didn't hit me back! Let me try this again." I hit him again to see if he would hit me; he didn't. I began to beat on him with my fist until I was almost out of breath. He tried to restrain me but he couldn't get a good grip on me. People were coming from all over to watch us fight. One guy was rolling down the street in a wheelchair! Finally, my husband picked me up and took me to my car and tried to shove me in it. As he did, I started kicking him with all the strength I had in my legs. He soon backed off of me and started walking towards his car. I followed him. I looked over at the woman and yelled, "Are you going with my husband?" "Don't answer her!" My husband yelled. "Are you going with my husband?" I yelled again. "Why don't you ask him?" She yelled back, "I'm asking you! I yelled back at her. "I thought you were saved!" She yelled to me.

What nerve she had to say that to me! "I ain't saved today!" I shouted back at her. By this time, her mother intervened and told me and my husband to leave or else she was going to call the police. I told her mom, "I ain't leaving till he leaves."

The woman then called my husband by his name and told him to leave. He closed the hood of his car, cranked it up and proceeded to drive off. I followed right behind him all the way to his dad's house. I didn't stop because I knew if I would have, we would be fighting again.

I decided to go to my dad's job. When I got there, I saw my dad's supervisor and asked to see my dad. Soon as daddy got to me, I broke down and started crying. All I could say between crying was, "I caught him! I caught him!" Daddy didn't say a word; he just hugged me and let me cry. After a few minutes of letting me cry my heart out and sweating really badly, daddy suggested that I get back in the car to cool off. He told me to go on home and that he would come by to check on me when he got off work.

When I got home, I got my baby out the car and walked down to my grandmother's house. Upon arriving at her house, I noticed that my mother-in-law's car was parked in the yard. I walked in the house and my mother-in-law said to me, "Hey Dianna, where you been?" "I just caught your son with another woman." "No, you didn't girl." She replied back. "Yes, I did."

"I was at work and the LORD spoke to me and told me to go see about Dianna. And now I know why." She replied with a puzzled looked in her eyes and a sound of sorrow in her voice. "Did you go by yourself?" My grandmother asked. "Yes ma'am I did."

Both my grandmother and my mother-in-law scolded me for going to the woman's house by myself and pleaded with me not to do that again. I told them that I didn't care about what I was doing at that time; all I wanted to do was to find my husband. I recapped the story of what had taken place and how I caught him. My mother-in-law was shocked that her son would have done that to me. She apologized for him and prayed for me. She told me that she loved me and I would always be her daughter-in-law no matter what. Soon after she left, my dad came by just as he promised he would.

On Wednesday morning, May 26, 1993, as I was preparing to go to my oldest son's graduation from Head Start, my grandmother told me that she had a dream that my husband would be calling me before the end of the month. I commented to her that the end of the month was only five days away and there was no way he was going to call me. She assured me it would come to pass. I shrugged it off because I didn't believe her.

Thursday night, after Bible study, I was at my grandmother's house on my knees praying to God and crying about the pain I had been enduring that week. About 12:30 AM, (Friday morning) the phone rang. I got off my knees and answered it. Guess who it was? You got it! It was my husband. It wasn't a call to tell me he was sorry or anything like that. He had a flat tire on his way to work and called me to see if he could borrow my car to go to work. What nerve he had! I told him there was no way he would use my car to ride that woman in.

We talked for a few minutes before he finally asked me to please pick him up and take him back to his father's house in Vidalia. I reluctantly agreed. I woke my grandmother up and informed her of the phone call.

She said to me, "I told you he would be calling you back before the end of the month, didn't I" I know what I'm talking about." "Yes, Grandma," I responded. "But it is only because he needs something from me, it ain't to get back with me,"

I left and met my husband. As I was on my way to his father's house, he asked me if he could come back to Glenwood with me. He apologized for the affair. He then went on to tell me that he and the woman were about to break up anyway.

Now that I look back on that statement, I see that I was second choice to him. Had he and that woman not been about to break up, he would not have came back to me. How naïve I was. I think about that night and shake my head; if only I knew then what I know now.

Needless to say, my husband and I reconciled. He promised me that he would never cheat on me again. He quit his job and broke off all contact with the woman. He began to treat me with the kindness of long ago. Because I loved him, I took him back and believed every word, empty promise and lie he told me.

After our reconciliation, he began to be a little more attentive to me. Not near as much as he was when I first met him, but more than he had been during the time of his affair. Our sex life improved a great deal. He was more patient with me and became concerned about me enjoying it. He wanted to make sure that it was as pleasurable for me as it was for him. It was at that point that I began to experience the joy of sex with my husband.

(I found out a few years later the Christmas shopping that I assumed my husband had done alone, was done by the woman he was going with. He had taken her shopping in my place.)

CHAPTER 12
My Beloved Dies
(No one left to love me)

The kindness from my husband was short-lived. His treatment toward me began to go back to the way it was before I found out about his affair. He never complimented me on anything I did. He became very negative towards me and spoke so much negativity into my life. My self-esteem was at an all-time low. He continued to drill into my head, no other man would want me and if they did, it was for what was between my legs. He had me thinking the worst of myself. Pretty or self-confidence was not a part of my vocabulary. I dropped from a size 10 down to a size 7 for no reason at all. For the next three years, we would continue to break up, make up and get back together. I was back and forth between my grandmother's house and my house. He was back and forth between his mother's house and my house.

Friday, March 15, 1996, one of the most devastating and overwhelming things in my life happened to me. I went to my grandmother's house to visit with her and found her lying on the floor dead. That was an awfully sad time in my life. The love of my life, my safe haven, my mother, my confidant, my comforter, my best friend had gone on to be with the LORD.

I don't know what I would have done without my grandmother in my life. She was my "everything." The only person in my life I knew that really loved me, faults and all. She was my "Mom." I felt very empty, isolated and alone. I cried for days, nights, weeks and months over her death. God was my strength through the entire ordeal. I went through a six-month depression after her death. I would have lost my mind had it not been for Him keeping me. Even to this day, there are moments when I still grieve over her death.

My husband didn't understand my pain and grief. He was not sympathetic for very long and after a while he bluntly told me to "Get over it." I attempted to go back to school, couldn't concentrate on it, so I quit. I tried to work, couldn't focus on the job, so I quit. In the meanwhile, our household bills started getting behind. I was then forced to stop grieving and go back to work full-time.

October of 1996, I applied for a job through a temporary agency and got hired. The very same week that I started work, our lights were disconnected. During that time, we lived next door to my dad and step-mother. I went next door and told my dad about my lights and he suggested that we run an extension cord from his house to mine. Also, he allowed me to take the food that I had in my refrigerator and freezer to his house so that it would not spoil. I was grateful for that. I would have felt better if he had just offered me to stay in the mobile home I grew up in that was still behind his house. But, he didn't offer, so I didn't ask.

I later found out it was against the law to use electricity from my dad's house. I informed him of that and he immediately disconnected the cord, leaving us in the dark once again.

Anyway, on a Friday afternoon (my lights had been out for a week at this point) my sister came to visit me. She told me that her husband had agreed to loan me the money to gets my lights reconnected. Thank God for Jesus! I decided that I would go and ask my dad for some money so that my family and I could stay at a hotel for the weekend. I wanted to do this so we could take good baths and be warm. Remember, my youngest son was a very sickly baby and I had to take special care so that he wouldn't get sick. He was three-years-old at this time.

My sister and I walked down to my dad's house and just as I was about to knock on the door, I could hear my step-mother talking. She was in mid-sentence when we heard her say, "Well, I hope she don't think she coming down here to stay."

My sister and I looked at each other. My sister mouthed to me, "She talking about you." "I know." I replied.

So we continued to listen to my step-mother and my dad converse back and forth for a few more moments. My sister couldn't take it anymore and opened the door abruptly without knocking. She and I walked in the house and let our parents know that we knew they were talking about me. I packed up all my food and every picture that I could find of me and my children and walked out the door. Just as I was about to slam the door shut, my step-mother said to me as she was sitting at the head of her dinner table, "God bless you."

"God, bless me?" I asked. "I don't know what God you're talking about because MY God don't act like that! I yelled back and slammed the door shut. As I was walking away tears began to stream down my face. I felt like my bones were on fire. I couldn't believe what I had just gone through and witnessed. My own father, yet again, failed to come through for me. He sat there and allowed my step-mother to talk about me and he just stood there and agreed with her. Is that love? Is that what God represents?

My mind went back to this portion of scripture:

And Jesus answering said, A certain man went down from Jerusalem to Jericho, and fell among thieves, which stripped him of his raiment, and wounded him, and departed, leaving him half dead. And by chance there came down a certain priest that way: and when he saw him, he passed by on the other side. And likewise a Levite, when he was at the place, came and looked on him, and passed by on the other side. But a certain Samaritan, as he journeyed, came where he was: and when he saw him, he had compassion on him, And went to him, and bound up his wounds, pouring in oil and wine, and set him on his own beast, and brought him to an inn, and took care of him. And on the morrow, when he departed, he took out two pence, and gave them to the host, and said unto him, Take care of him; and whatsoever thou spendest more, when I come again, I will repay thee. Which now of these three, thinkest thou, was neighbor unto him that fell among thieves? Luke 10:30-36

You talk about being disappointed and hurt all over again. As I stated earlier, I felt I had no one to depend on, I was alone. I don't feel my dad and my step-mother had compassion for me and the situation my family were in.

I missed my grandmother more than ever. At the time, I knew in my heart that I couldn't bear to go and stay in her house. I was still grieving over her death. I never even considered it, not one time. If I went inside of her home, I felt like I would see her lying on the floor just as I had when I found her. I refused to go back in her home for many years. It would be August 2010 before I would finally make the choice to step foot in her house again.

CHAPTER 13
MY AFFAIR

At my new job, I met a man who had a close family member that was dying from a terminal illness. He and I became very good friends. He began to tell me about the problems he was having in his home. I began to look forward to going to work every day, just so I could see him and talk with him.

My conscious told me that what I was doing was wrong, but I convinced myself that I was only friends with the guy because of his dying family member. I shared with him the details of my grandmother's death, and expressed that I knew how it felt to have no one to turn to. I wanted to be the shoulder he leaned on, the confidant he could talk to, etc. I did everything I could to justify the relationship with him. In my mind, I felt it would be "safe" to be his friend. I now know that was a trick of the enemy.

About seven months later, the man's family member passed away. I promised myself that I would be there for him during his grieving process. I didn't want him to feel alone, as I knew firsthand how awful it felt. Not that he needed me, but I still wanted to be there as a "friend" to him. I made myself available to him. My husband had no knowledge of the new friendship I had developed with this guy.

The following month, my husband and I had another one of our major arguments. I don't even remember what it was about, but it made me angry enough to move out. Since I had a new found friend, it was the more reason for me to do so. I packed my bags and my two boys and I moved in with my sister and her husband. I couldn't wait to get to work the next morning to share the news of what happened between my husband and me with my friend. When I told my friend, without hesitation, he asked me if it would be okay for him to come see me. I eagerly told him yes.

Later that evening, my friend and I were sitting outside in the car. He began to talk to me from his heart (at least I thought it was coming from his heart) He told me how beautiful I was. He told me all the positive things about myself that I had somehow pushed down into my subconscious mind. He placed me on a pedestal and I began to feel good about myself once again. As I started to speak in response to what he said, he placed a soft, unexpected kiss on the side of my mouth. I was speechless. It literally took my breath away. It felt really good to be kissed by my friend.

Day after day, he found a way to give me compliments, making me feel better about myself. His words boosted my self-esteem; I saw myself in a different way. Although, the devil meant it for bad, I can see the good that came out of it. I regained my self-esteem that was previously been torn down by my husband.

A few months later, I reconciled with my husband and moved back home. But, my relationship with my friend did not stop. In fact, it flourished even more.

I decided to go back to school. I enrolled in evening classes. During my evening break, my friend would come visit me at school. Oftentimes, he would bring me dinner that he cooked. I began to fall in love with him and the things he was saying and doing for me. Or was I falling "in lust" with him?

As you may have already guessed, I had a love/lust affair with my friend. Yes, I knew it was wrong, but I felt it was beautiful at the same time. He treated me with the utmost respect. He took me out to the nicest restaurants and the best motels in town. He gave me roses, just because. He made me feel loved, wanted and special. Because we worked together, we would take our breaks together and eat lunch together on a daily basis. He would bring breakfast to work for me and buy my lunch every day. Sometimes on our lunch break we would go to a local park and play basketball together. He introduced me to a new life; entirely different than what I was used to.

Eventually, my guilt got the best of me and I told my husband about my affair; but it was hopeless, and there was nothing he could do about it. I had fallen in love with another man. I suppose my husband was hurt, but it did not change my feelings about my affair. My husband had oftentimes said to me that he knew I was going to get him back for him having an affair on me. I tried to explain to him, that was not the case at all.

The earlier part of the following year, I decided to leave my husband and find a place of my own. I was still having my affair and had no intentions of stopping. The day I started moving out and began to claim the furniture that was mine, my husband attempted to beat me. He started yelling at me about what I could and could not take. I had had enough of his beatings; I retaliated. I ran to the kitchen and grabbed a knife out of the drawer. I walked towards him while holding the knife in the air pointed directly at him. I shouted to him that he better not put his hands on me ever again and I meant it. He looked shocked, backed away from me and left the room.

I was glad to be free from my husband. My friend would come and stay at my house for days at a time. Then all of a sudden, he would go missing and I wouldn't hear from him. I didn't like that at all. I started hearing rumors that my friend had numerous women that he was sleeping with and I felt like a fool. I found myself getting in my car and riding through all types of neighborhoods looking for him in the middle of the night. I knew deep in my heart, I didn't want to live like that and I certainly didn't want my children to be a part of that either.

December 26, 1998, as I was asleep in bed next to my friend the Holy Spirit woke me up and began to talk to me. The lifestyle that I was living was contrary to the WORD of God. This man I was sleeping with was my enemy, not my friend. Sure, my flesh craved the affection; but in my heart I knew it was wrong. I thought about what Paul wrote to the Church of Galatia in Galatians 5:17, *"For the flesh lusted against the Spirit and the Spirit against the flesh; and these are contrary the one to the other: so that ye cannot do the things that you would."* I got out of bed, picked up the phone book and looked up my sister's pastor's phone number. I had never met her, but I knew at that very moment I needed prayer and a personal WORD from God.

I called my sister's pastor and explained my situation to her. She told me that my flesh would desire both my husband and my friend because they were both fulfilling different needs that I had. She explained to me that the relationship with my friend was wrong and I needed to end it. She also stated that I needed to make a decision on whether or not I wanted to save my marriage. She prayed for me and asked God to give me direction on which way to go. In my heart, I wanted my husband; not my friend.

During the separation from my husband, he had gone on to meet someone else. I didn't know much about the woman, but I was determined to get my husband back. I called him on the phone and told him that I loved him and wanted to work on our marriage. I even took it upon myself to go see his new girlfriend at her house. Yes, I went to the woman's house alone, but not to start an argument with her. I wanted to find out just how serious the relationship was between her and my husband. She was hesitant to let me in, but I explained to her that I only wanted to talk to her. Reluctantly, she allowed me inside her home. *As I am sitting here typing this, again, I am shaking my head in disbelief. I was a pretty brave woman and that woman was crazy for letting me into her house!*

She offered me a seat and as I sat down, I noticed a big beautiful bouquet of light pink roses on the table. I commented on how beautiful they were. She looked at me and told me that my husband had given them to her and that I could have them if I wanted them. Although I got a little upset, I said, "No honey, he bought them for you." She then went on to tell me that he had purchased her a pair of expensive athletic shoes for Christmas. I was sitting there almost in shock. I held my composure really well. How could this man buy this woman, he hardly knew, flowers and shoes? He hadn't bought me flowers since before we got married and had only bought me one pair of cheap sandals!

The woman went on to explain to me that she and my husband were just friends. She said she kissed him but had not had sex with him. I'm not sure if I believed her or not. She then told me that she was no longer interested in him and that I could have him back. I told her that I would leave that choice up to my husband. I left her house and went to my sister-in-law's house to see my husband. He had been living with her at the time. I informed him of where I had been. He was furious with me and cursed me out. I left.

December 31, 1998, on my way to Watch Night Service, I went by my former friend's house to take the remainder of the clothes he left at my house to him. There were very little words exchanged between us. He acted as if he didn't care about me anymore and thanked me for bringing the clothes by. I left and went to church.

A couple of days after New Year's Day, my husband called me and told me that he had made the decision to get back together with me and work on our marriage. I happily agreed with him. Our reunion started out wonderful. I felt like I was falling in love with him all over again. I can honestly say that I felt like a newlywed. What a wonderful feeling it was.

I will never forget, Sunday, January 31, 1999, he and I watched the Super Bowl together. It was between the Denver Broncos and the Atlanta Falcons. It would be my first time watching a football game, but certainly not my last. I enjoyed watching the game and spending time with him.

The following Valentine's Day, he came home with a beautiful teddy bear arrangement. The very next weekend, he bought me a dozen cream-colored roses! He was on a roll and I loved it.

September of 1999, I graduated from Southeastern Technical College with a degree in Word Processing. I was proud of this accomplishment. Out of every obstacle that attempted to get in the way of my schooling, I overcame.

CHAPTER 14
FINDING MY OTHER "MOM"

February of 2000, I began to think about the other woman my father had been engaged to before he married my step-mother. I remembered the lady somewhat. I remember visiting with her and going to church with her on at least one occasion. I also remember the lady having a son of her own. I think he and I may have been around the same age. My grandmother had told me a lot about how nice the lady was and how much she loved me, my sisters and my brother. She had also told me the lady's first and last name; I never forgot it. I set out on a mission to find her.

Since I knew her name and knew what town she lived in during the time my father dated her, I started there. I looked in the phone book and searched for her last name. I had decided that I would call every person with that last name and ask for her each time. As fate would have it, there was only one person in the phone book from that town, listed with the same last name as hers. I called the number, but no one answered, so I left a voicemail stating who I was and the reason for my call.

One day later, I got a return call. It was an elderly lady who called me. She began to explain to me that I had called the right number and that she was married to the lady's father that I was looking for. She sounded so excited and explained to me that she had mentioned my phone call to her husband and he confirmed that I was telling the truth. She went on to tell me that the lady I was looking for lived in another state and she would surely give her my message and my phone number.

The very next day, when I got home from work, I had a voicemail message on my phone. It was the lady I looking for. She started off the message by saying, "Hi Dianna, this is your mom. I have oftentimes wondered how my babies were doing. I have been praying for you all and have always loved you. I have missed you so much. When Grandma told me that you called, I couldn't believe it! Thank you for looking for me. Please call me as soon as you get this message."

As I was listening to the message, tears of joy came to my eyes! I was so happy that I found my other "Mom." With both anticipation and excitement, I picked up the phone and called her. She quickly answered and began to pledge her never ending love for me, my sisters and my brother. She told me about the short courtship between her and my father and how she kept us and fell in love with us. She told me how my father gave her an engagement ring, and then right after her bridal shower told her that he had decided to marry someone else. She went on to explain to me how she begged him to let her keep us as her own children; that he could go on with his life. My father had initially agreed to that, according to her, but eventually changed his mind.

I was very amazed at the love she declared to still have for me and my sisters. I started wondering why my dad broke off the engagement with her and married my step-mother only a few days after. So, I questioned her about it. She told me that my dad broke up with her on a Saturday and was married to my step-mother the following Tuesday! My father told her that my step-mother told him that the LORD told her that he was her husband and that he was suppose to marry her and help her raise her children.

Now, as I look back at that statement, that is EXACLTY what my father did. He married my step-mother and he truly helped her raise her children.

I eagerly shared the news with my sisters and they were both equally as excited to talk with our new "Mom" as I was. We would all get on a three-way, four-way call or whatever way we could and talk with her for hours on end. Our new "Mom" told us how she returned all the bridal shower gifts to her friends and that she had to have counseling because of the devastation my father put her through. I don't know if he knows or understands the emotional anguish he caused her so many years ago.

I eventually met the elderly lady I had spoken with initially. She was just the sweetest person you ever wanted to meet. She met me at the door with open arms and kisses on my cheek. She insisted that I call her "Grandma." I met her husband and he too was just as gracious. He insisted that I call him "Grandpa".

I was so happy that I had found our new "Mom" and new "Grandparents." We planned our reunion meeting which took place in July of 2000. What a reunion it was. She came up to where we lived and my sisters and I cooked a big dinner welcoming her and her children. She had one biological son and three adopted children, two boys and one girl. When she saw us, she had tears in her eyes. She hugged all three of us at the same time and had a present for each of us. She gave me and my middle sister a doll, and my youngest sister a stuffed animal. Before we were finished, we all had tears of joy in our eyes. We embraced our new siblings as they embraced us. What a happy reunion it was.

Our "Mom" loved on our children and told them that she was their Grandmother. Upon her return home, she sent all of them gifts. I thank God for the newfound joy He had given to me and my sisters.

We have continued to stay in touch with her and each of us have visited and stayed with her at her home.

CHAPTER 15
MY "LIVE" BABY DOLL

Things between my husband and I went very well for the next three years. I have oftentimes heard people say that "affairs" make your marriage stronger. I am in NO way condoning cheating on your mate, but in my case, there was a small truth to it at the time. However, I give no credit to the devil. What my husband and I did was very wrong. For the Bible distinctly says, *"Flee fornication. Every sin that a man doeth is without the body; but he that committeth fornication sinneth against his own body."* 1 Corinthians *6:18*. But to God be all the Glory. I thank Him for His Grace, Goodness and Mercy.

In July 2001, since things were going well for us, my husband and I decided that we would have another baby. We had two boys already but my husband wanted a girl. I told him that it didn't matter to me what it was just as long as it was healthy. My husband prayed and prayed for a girl.

It would be November 2001 before I would conceive. During my entire pregnancy, my husband treated me like a queen. He treated me with such care, kindness and understanding. There was nothing that I wanted that he didn't get for me. I almost wished my pregnancy could have lasted longer than the 37 weeks that it did.

When I went to the doctor to confirm my pregnancy, he gave me the due date of July 26, 2002. Now if you remember from an earlier chapter, my Mom was buried on this date. I knew that I didn't want to have my baby on that date. I didn't want to have to associate my baby's birth with my Mother's death in any way.

At my 37 week checkup, I had already started to dilate, which is normal. My doctor asked me if I wanted to go ahead and give birth early. He informed me that my baby was developed enough to be born healthy. He then suggested the date of July 18, 2002. This date was also unacceptable for me because this was when my Mother died. I asked my doctor if he could induce me on July 17 instead. He agreed. July 17, 2002, I gave birth to a beautiful 7 lbs. 8 oz. baby girl.

I'm sure that everyone who has a child says that their child is the most beautiful baby in the world and that is exactly how I felt. You see, as a child, I do not remember my father ever buying me a baby doll. Almost every little girl wants a doll to play with…my step-sisters and half-sisters had plenty, but not me nor my sisters. If we played with dolls, we had to sneak the dolls and go off in a room so that no one could see us. As I am writing this, I am shaking my head once again because it is hard to believe, but it's true. I can remember sneaking my oldest step-sister's doll and going in the bathroom to play with it. No child should ever have to go through that, but I did. God knew my heart once again and He, my loving Father, blessed me with my very own "live" baby doll. I got to love her, dress her up, bathe her etc. You get the picture……

My dad was unable to come visit me in the hospital because he was at home sick. Once I was home, he came to see me and his new grand-daughter. As soon as he walked through the door, I said to him, "I finally got my baby doll now."

I am not quite sure how that made him feel, but I wanted him to know that he didn't have to buy me one. I guess I was being sarcastic towards him, but that was a hurt that I had carried for so long. Even to this day I can't say that I feel sorry for what I said, because it is true.

My new "Mom" sent me a box of clothes for my baby and a little stuffed lamb that played, "Mary Had a Little Lamb" as it moved its head. Believe it or not, my now 10-year-old daughter sleeps with it to this very day.

CHAPTER 16
My Paternity Questioned

One night, I went to visit my father. He and I were outside having a conversation and somehow we started talking about my baby brother and his death. During the conversation, my father insinuated that he did not think that my baby brother was his child. A look of total disbelief came across my face. I then suggested to my father that he could have my brother's body exhumed and have a paternity test performed to ease his suspicion. Then I asked him if he thought me or my sisters were his children. You will not believe me, but he told me he wasn't sure about us either. He said the one he was most unsure of was my youngest sister. So I asked him if he was sure that my half-sisters were his. He replied, "Oh yeah, I know they are mine!" You talking about hurt; boy I was hurt. Tears began to stream down my face as I told my father that I refuse to let him tarnish the good image that I had of my Mother. I angrily got into my car and drove off.

I left his house crying so badly; I could hardly see the road. Once I got home, I called both my sisters on the three-way and told them what had just transpired between my father and me. They were both in shock and utter disbelief just as I was. We began to come to the conclusion that this was the reason our father allowed us to be treated the way we had been treated during our childhood. Inside of him, he secretly believed that we were not his children. I have no idea why he felt that way or why he chose to share that information with me.

My sisters and I decided that we wanted paternity tests done between us and our father. I ordered the tests, but I refused to pay a dime for it. I wrote my father a long letter and mailed it to him along with the paternity test. My youngest sister also wrote a letter to him expressing the hurt she felt.

A few weeks later, my father came over to my house to visit me. He began to say how sorry he was for saying that he wasn't sure if he was my father. He explained to me that while he was in Texas, my mother came to live with him. She was not pregnant at the time, but became pregnant with me and delivered while she was there. My dad pleaded with me to forgive him. Needless to say, we did not go through with the paternity tests, but I will always have that doubt in my mind.

He probably visited with me for about 2 or 3 hours. When he got ready to leave, I walked him to the door. Lo and behold, I looked at his car and there sat my step-mother in the front seat. I spoke to her, but in my mind I was both shocked and concerned that she had been sitting out there the entire time. I don't know what she was thinking and at that point I really didn't care.

(I would like to say that my step-mother had told me years ago that my uncle, my mother's oldest sister's husband, was my father. She made sure to tell me that I looked just liked one of my 1st cousins and said they were my sisters and brothers.

Every time someone says to me that I look like a family member on my father's side, my father will say to me, "That's confirmation." Or if someone says that my sons look like him, he will say the same thing. Even to this day, he makes the same comment. Now, that makes me think that my father is still unsure that he is my biological father. Why would he continue to say that? It burns me up inside every time I hear him say, "That's confirmation." I try not to let it bother me, but it does and I have decided that if he says it to me one more time, he is going to know how I feel about it.)

CHAPTER 17
REMOVING THE SCAB FROM THE SORE

For the next few years, my relationship with my husband began to become a roller coaster ride all over again. We would get along for a while and then we would be mad with each other for awhile. I was in church, he was not. It was another rough patch in our marriage. Nevertheless, my faith in God continued to grow.

One afternoon in July of 2006, my middle sister and I were on the phone with one of my step-cousins (my step-mother's niece). We were having a very good conversation when my cousin asked me why we never kept in touch with our oldest step-brother. I got quiet and my sister piped up, "Well Dianna, I guess it is time to let the cat out of the bag." I thought for a moment and reluctantly agreed with her. I began to share with my cousin about the raping and the molestation I suffered at the hands of my step-brother as a child.

My cousin was outraged. I could hear the anger in her voice as she tearfully apologized for the actions of her "blood" cousin; my step-brother. She could not believe it. I told her that I had no reason to lie on him and that I was tired of keeping the "Family Secret" anyway. She asked me if I minded if she called my oldest step-brother on the phone and confronted him about the molestation and rape. I told her it was ok by me. I was truly hoping that she would get the truth out of him once and for all.

A few days later, my cousin called me back and said that my step-bother denied everything and told her not to let her mouth be a garbage can. He told her that I was a liar and not to believe anything that I told her. I choked up and held back the tears. I could tell by the tone of her voice that she really didn't want to have that conversation with me. So, we ended the phone call quickly and it would be years before I would speak with her again.

Once I hung up the phone, I burst into tears. My husband and daughter came to the room where I was. He asked me what was wrong; I tried to explain to him about the phone call. He told my daughter not to bother me. He did not try to comfort me at all. He shook his head at me and walked away. I cried even more. I needed him, yet he wasn't there for me. He didn't care.

I got off the couch and went into the bathroom to call my youngest sister. I began to try and explain to her what had just happened. As I began to talk to her, I became overwhelmed with emotion and started crying uncontrollably. I hung up the phone and plopped down on the floor. I was crying so hard that I started to hyperventilate. It was like I was reliving the pain of the raping and the molestation all over again. All kinds of thoughts were running through my mind. How dare he deny what he did to me? How dare he call me a liar? Would people think that I was a liar and would actually make it all up? All I could say out loud was, "Lord Jesus Help Me!" "LORD Jesus, pleeeaassee take this pain away" "Please Jesus Help me!" I had no idea that I was still hurting that badly.

As I was sitting on the floor of the bathroom crying, my sweet little baby girl, who was 4 years old at the time, came and sat down on my lap. She put her little arms around my neck and started crying with me. Isn't that just like God? He, through my daughter, comforted me right then and there. He let me know that He was with me; He loved me and He was going to take care of me.

Shortly after, my sister arrived at my house. She came to see about me. She hugged me and prayed for peace in my heart. She assured me that everything was going to be alright and that God, our Father, had my back. She told me not to worry and to give it all to Jesus.

The Bibles says in Matthew 11:28-30, *Come unto Me, all ye that labour and are heavy laden, and I will give you rest. Take my yoke upon you, and learn of me; for I am meek and lowly in heart: and ye shall find rest unto your souls. For my yoke is easy, and my burden is light.*

When my oldest son came home (he was 19 at the time) and saw me crying, he wanted to know what was going on. My sister and I explained to him what happened. He became very angry and insisted on calling my step-brother. Some kind of way, we got my step-brother's phone number and my son called him. He began to ask my step-brother if what I had accused him of was true. My step-brother told him that he doesn't talk to children and if I wanted to talk to him, then I should call him myself. This made my son angrier. Some harsh words were said and he hung up the phone. Then he started crying out of anger and hurt for me. So I had to comfort him. My middle sister found out what had happened and she called my step-brother and cursed him out.

Later that night, I called my "new" Mom and informed her of the day's events. She listened to me without interrupting. When I was done talking she asked me, "Dianna, have you ever told him how you feel about that?"

I answered her, "No ma'am I haven't." Then I went on to tell her about the time when I did get a chance to talk with him, how I tried desperately to get him to apologize and he wouldn't.

Then she said to me, "Why don't you write him a letter and tell him exactly how you feel?"

I thought about it for a few seconds, and then I said, "That's a good idea; I will do it tomorrow."

She then said to me, "Make sure you have the letter certified so that you will know that he got it." I said, "Ok," and then we ended our conversation.

I typed the letter up the next day and sent it off certified mail. This is the letter that I wrote to him in its entirety. These are the original words of the letter, with the exception of omitting any names to protect identities. There is some explicit language in the letter.

August 3, 2006

Hi,

First of all, it is your choice to whether or not you continue reading this letter or not. I have also sent a copy of this same letter to your mother and my daddy so there will be no discrepancies about it.

The reason I sent it certified is to be sure that all of you received it.

I know that you probably want to know why I exposed your dirty secret to your cousin. She called me. She and I got into a discussion about how bad she felt about the way we had been treated by your mother when we were younger. I didn't initiate that part of the conversation. (She isn't the only one of your family members who expressed how they felt about us being mistreated by your mother, plenty more have come forth, plenty of them.)

Anyway, she asked me if the children, "us" kept in touch with each other. I bluntly told her "NO" and that you would never in your life call me or come by my house. She asked me why and I told her the unadulterated truth. I didn't add anything nor take anything away from it. I was as honest with her as I could be. She asked me if I cared if she asked you about it and I told her "No" I didn't care if she did or not. Her mouth isn't the "garbage can" you called it and I didn't tell her any "trash" as you put it. I told her that I went to you and you never admitted that you raped and molested me continually throughout your entire teenage life. I apologized to you, knowing that I did nothing wrong, just to get you to apologize to me and you would not do it and you haven't done it to this day.

You want to know why this keeps coming up; it is because it is something that **I** live with **EVERY SINGLE DAY** of my life. It has affected **EVERY SINGLE RELATIONSHIP** I have had with my past boyfriends and in my marriage. **YOU SCARRED ME FOR LIFE!!!!!!! AND YOU DON'T HAVE OR FEEL ANY REMORSE FOR WHAT YOU DID!!!!!**

You made me lick your butt-hole for hours it seemed like…you made me suck your penis "like it was a bottle"…you ejaculated on me and told me to go bathe because I could get pregnant…you had sex with me and I remember the exact day that my hymen was broken because my panties were blood-stained the next morning when I got up. You even made me kiss you as if I was enjoying what you did to me. <u>**YOU WERE ONE SICK BASTARD AND YOU PROBABLY STILL ARE.**</u> To this day, my uterus isn't shaped right because of what you did to me. You lied to MY daddy about molesting me and sadly he believed YOU because **he wanted to believe a lie instead of the truth**. If he really wanted to know the truth, he would have come to me and asked me. When he found out, he told your mama and she took up for you. She told daddy that I probably asked for it. <u>**ALL OF YOU ARE JUST PLAIN CRAZY!!!!!!**</u> I even remember the time when you put me and my baby brother in the bathroom and turned the light out and made me change his cloth diaper in the dark. I would put my hand inside the diaper so I would stick him with the pin and you made me redo it again and again. I realized you wanted me to stick him, so I did and he cried and then you were satisfied and left me alone. My brother is dead today because of your mother and my daddy's neglect of not taking him to the doctor. Daddy has tried to blame my baby brother's death on some medication that he got into at grandma's house. Let me tell you something, if he was going to have a reaction to the medication, he would have had it right there and then, not two weeks later. You being a so-called doctor know that it doesn't take medication that long to react to a child's body, especially an adult dose of medication. His death has been swept under the rug as if he never lived. You all can continue to live a lie if you want to and deny the truth and pretend everything is ok. It is not and never will be until some confessions and true forgiveness is done within the family.

112

I am not apologizing for my sister for calling you and cursing you out. I am not apologizing for my son calling you and being concerned about me. Just so you know, they all know the dirty details of what you put me through. Your siblings are probably the ones that don't know the full details. Another thing, when I went to your brother (yes, he molested me too, he didn't have sex with me…he just fondled me) he was just as humble as he could be. He admitted it and apologized to me from the bottom of his heart. We hugged and I told him that I loved him like a brother. But you, you said you don't remember and that we were just kids. **YOU ARE A BIG LIAR!!!!!** Keep on believing that. You must don't have no conscious at all.

I got the message that you all have moved on with your lives and have let go of the past and we are the only ones holding on to it. We were the victims. We were the ones who got hurt. We were the ones who got mistreated. Yes, we all have been going through for 30 plus years and it won't go away until some true confessions and forgiveness takes place as I said earlier.

Your mother and my daddy are in denial about the past too. Your mother thinks that she did everything she could for us and loved us like we were her own children. God in heaven above knows that is not the truth. She hated us with a passion. She never wanted us; all she wanted was daddy. And that is the truth. And daddy, I don't know what he was thinking about when he married her. I agree with what my sister said when she said she wished daddy wouldn't have married your mother. I have wished that many times, but we can't change a decision that he made. But through it all, we found out that he loved you and your siblings more than he loved us. I say that because, he never prosecuted you when I told him the truth about what you done to me. He never took me to the doctor to be examined or to a psychologist to see if I needed counseling or anything. He protected you, your mama and your name at my expense. He wanted to keep peace with your mother and with you rather than get justice for his own daughter. So that in itself lets me know that he really doesn't love me. He just tolerates me because I am his BLOOD daughter. God is still good no matter what has happened in my life. The enemy is and always has been up to no good. It is his job to steal, kill and destroy and that is what he has done to my sisters and I. We are still hurting from the wounds of the past. Yes, we want to get over it and let it go, but it just hasn't gone away. We have been rejected ALL our lives by your family including my daddy. We have always been considered the outsiders or the black sheep of the family. Daddy thinks that we were brainwashed and that we hallucinated a lot of things that were told to him. He is delusional himself. There is no way on God's green earth that he loves us, he can't possibly love us and think that way about us.

I know that you all didn't like my grandmother. She was a woman who spoke her piece and loved you anyway. She was the only one who showed us genuine love. I don't care what you, your mama or daddy has said about her. She loved me and my siblings with all her heart and she wanted what was best for us. Daddy should have just made the decision to leave us with her, but he didn't and we can't change that. I loved my grandmother and resent the fact that you called her "mouthing" and told my sister, "Yeah, your dead grandma." Grandma was trying to look out for our best interest. She knew how your grandmother (a tarot card reader) and your mother were and she didn't want us to be part of your family just like you all didn't want us to be a part of it either. NOBODY brainwashed me and I have never had a hallucination of any sort. If anything, daddy was the one brainwashed and still is. Only daddy and God know how he really feels inside. I personally think it was the biggest mistake of his life. But, there is nothing I can do about it. They are married for life and I am glad they are sticking with each other through all of the things that have happened. I am hurt by it, but also glad to know that some marriages can endure regardless of how many storms come through. My hat is off to them.

I found out that it was daddy's decision to put us out in the trailer. What in the world could he have been thinking at the time? I don't know. I mean his own flesh and blood in a trailer with no running water, no working bathroom and very, I mean very little heat in the winter. That in itself was child abuse because it was neglect. We were cut off from you all in the very beginning. Your mother would leave food in your sister's room during the summer so that they could have something to eat, and wouldn't leave us anything. (I confronted her about that she has amnesia just like you do) She claims she doesn't remember that. And you, when you were home, would cook you something and eat right in front of us knowing how hungry we were. The cornflakes and milk in the house were you all's and we were **dared** to touch it, by you. You were a very mean person and you had to take my innocence away from me on top of all that. Your mama was mean to us too. She wouldn't let us go and visit the one person who loved us. All I can do is just shake my head in despair. I don't see how you, your mama and daddy can say that none of what we remember is true. You all can say that it is a lie or whatever you want. If you feel that that is not the truth, then the real truth needs to be told by the one who knows the truth, the whole truth and nothing but the truth. **YOU ARE ALL IN DENIAL AND I AM SORRY FOR YOU.**

I just want to get past this. I really, really, really, want to get past this so I can go on with my life. I have been hurting for a very, very long time and God knows why this has come up again. Maybe this time, it will finally be resolved. I am getting everything off my chest. Yes, I refused to call you and I told my son that it will be a cold day in hell before I did. So, instead, I decided to write it all down so I could pray about it before I put it in the mail and so that I wouldn't be interrupted while I am saying what I have to say. This in itself is a part of my healing process. I know it is. Telling my perpetrator how I feel about what he did to me. That is something I never have got a chance to do until now. It is up to you to own up to what you did, apologize and ask for forgiveness.

115

I am trying not to hold any resentment against you. It is very, hard, but I try every day. I have asked God to take the pain and hurt away. I refuse to live the rest of my life like this. I just can't. It is not healthy for me to keep holding onto the past like I have. And your sister can easily say let the past stay in the past because she didn't go through what I went through. As I said earlier, ALL OF YOU ARE LIVING IN DENIAL. That is the path that you all have chosen to take and I am sorry for you.

I know I am not where I should be in Christ, but I am striving to make it into the Kingdom of God. I am not perfect; I have made my share of mistakes. When I know that, I don't run from them, I confront them head on.

All I have ever wanted was to feel part of a real family. I have yet to feel that with you and your mama. It is just not there. Daddy isn't in the middle. He is on your side, so you got him in your corner fighting for you. Who have I got? I have Jesus and I know beyond a shadow of a doubt that he loves me.

So you continue on living a fruitful life. I just wanted to let you know once and for all how I honestly feel about you. I don't hate you; I hate what you did to me. I don't hate your mother; I hate how she treated me and my sisters. I don't hate daddy; I hate that him being a man let that happen and did nothing about it. I just have to pray to God to put genuine love in my heart for each of you. I don't want to die and go to hell for nobody.

I have told your mother that she and I would never have a mother-daughter relationship, but there is still time for us to be friends. And the same goes for you. I have a forgiving heart. And I forgive you for what you did to me. And I forgive your mother and my daddy for protecting you and not me. I am not a bad person. It is in my heart to forgive, my grandmother taught me that. She always told us that we have to love no matter what. And that seed is planted in my heart.

Take care and be blessed,

Dianna ~

About two weeks later, the letter came back to me unopened with a stamped impression "Return to Sender." He had refused delivery of the letter. That was another blow to my heart. This time I didn't cry, I had a plan. I became angry and wanted revenge right then and there. So I made up my mind that I would print out multiple copies of the letter and send it to as many family members as I could. I would expose him for what he did to me. And that is exactly what I did. I cannot tell you how many letters I printed and mailed out. I mailed them to his cousins and my cousins. I even emailed the letter to the ones whose email addresses I had at the time. I also mailed a copy to both of his neighbors because I wanted them to know that they lived next to a child molester. Any of my family members or friends who came by my house, I let them read the letter. I sent one to my step-mother's sisters too. I was a very angry woman.

How many of you know that was the wrong thing for me to do? I listened to my flesh and took vengeance into my own hands. Can I say that I was happy for what I did? No, I wasn't. I felt really bad after I was finished distributing the letter.

In Romans 12:17-21 it says, *"Recompense to no man evil for evil. Provide things honest in the sight of all men. If it be possible, as much as lieth in you, live peaceably with all men. Dearly beloved, avenge not yourselves, but rather give place unto wrath: for it is written, VENGEANCE IS MINE; I WILL REPAY, saith the LORD. Therefore, IF THINE ENEMY HUNGER, FEED HIM, IF HE THIRST, GIVE HIM DRINK; FOR IN SO DOING THOU SHALT HEAP COALS OF FIRE ON HIS HEAD. Be not overcome of evil, but overcome evil with good.*

All I wanted was an apology. That is all I ever desired from my step-brother, acknowledgement and an apology.

CHAPTER 18
DIANNA, I DISOWN YOU

The letters that I distributed caused so much chaos and havoc for my step-brother and my step-mother. People that I spoke with were somewhat shocked at the accusations I made against my step-brother. Some even wondered why it was all coming out now and what the point of it was.

In October of 2006, a phone call was made. I can't remember if I made the call or if the call was made to me. At any rate, my step-mother and I had a very heated argument. It started off by her telling me that I was a liar and that I was going to burst hell wide open. Yes, those were the words she said to me, but I immediately told her that I knew I was going to heaven. She asked me why I sent those letters to her family and that nothing I did was going to break them up. Of course, that wasn't my intention, but she made sure to tell me that she had already talked to everyone and told them that I had told a bunch of lies about her son.

She talked about how she didn't like my grandmother and that my real mother's family turned us against her. She went on about how she tried to do the right thing by us. She said to me, "When you were 4 years old, you told me to my face that I wasn't your mama! I know you had to get that from them. Everything you did, both your sisters followed right behind you! Y'all were some bad, disobedient children. I hated the way y'all acted when y'all would come back from your grandma's!"

Now, I want to say something here, if a four- year-old child that I had to raise told me that I was not her mama, I would have tried my best to win her over with love. I would have hugged her and assured her that no matter what or who I was to her, I would love her anyway. Do you agree? I couldn't believe that she had held on to that one statement all of her life. She really took that personally for her to remember that all those years later. I have no remembrance of telling her that she wasn't my mother, but in essence, I told the truth. The conversation went on for almost two hours with her and me going back and forth about the past. I asked her if she loved my daddy when she married him. She told me that two people don't have to love each other to get married. "The love can come later." She went on to tell me that my daddy asked her soon after my mom died to go out with him and she turned him down because she was afraid that people would say they had been going together all the while. Then she said something to me that literally freed me. She said, "Dianna, I disowned you. That's right, I told your daddy a long time ago that I disowned you! I disowned all three of you girls! And your daddy's on the other end listening right now and he knows it's the truth!"

At first, I was shocked at what I had just heard. I asked myself, "Did she really just say she disowned me?" I thought about that thing for a few seconds. Then, I began to feel all happy inside. Before I knew it, I said to her, "Thank God! Thank you Jesus I don't have to pretend anymore!!! You just don't know what you have done for me! I am free!!!!!" I can't even begin to express the sense of freedom I felt. The feeling was so intense, I felt like I could have grown a pair of wings and flown away. I felt relief all over my body! It was surreal.

Again, my father did not take up for me nor come to my defense. He listened in silence as my step-mother and I went at it over the phone. Why didn't he say anything? Why did he let the conversation go on as long as it did? Why did he allow her to call me a liar? His silence to me was in agreement with what she was saying. We talked until her phone started beeping and went dead.

I immediately called both my sisters on three-way to fill them in on what had just happened. They were both shocked. Neither one of them could believe that daddy didn't say a word. But we all felt a sense of relief.

That same year, on November 25, 2006, we threw ourselves our first birthday party ever. We celebrated our newly found lives of freedom that night. We had a blast! We invited close family and friends and celebrated "Us" for the first time.

I would like to add here that several pictures were taken during and after the party. When I went to pick the pictures up from the photographer, I saw myself as being beautiful for the first time ever in my life. I told the photographer, "This can't be me."
He responded, "The camera took what it saw."

CHAPTER 19
THE BREAK-UP

During the entire time of me writing the letter to my step-brother and the phone call between me and my step-mother, my marriage was suffering terribly. I was so focused on myself and my emotions that I had no time for my husband. We began to argue on an everyday basis it seemed. We didn't get along at all.

I had finally had enough and I moved out. I filed for a divorce. My husband refused to sign the papers. It seemed that my life began a downward spiral after that. Nothing was going right for me. My job was going well, and then all of a sudden, I became the enemy to my boss. He wanted me to do something that was not ethical and I refused to do it, so he made my job hard for me to do. Eventually, I lost my job because of it.

Here I was living a single life again with no job to support myself. I had stopped going to church and I just existed. I had no idea what I was going to do or where I was going to live. I was living a very lonely life. I went to Atlanta and stayed with my sister almost 2 months to look for a job. Nothing was working out for me. I had left God out.

Financially, I could not make it on my own. So I moved back home with my husband. We were still not getting along. We didn't even share the same bedroom. I remember feeling a sense of hopelessness; like my freedom was gone again. I went from being on a high to feeling very low, even worse than I felt before all the chaos happened with the exposure of the little dirty family secrets. I almost wished I could turn back the hands of time to change things. But in my heart I knew I couldn't.

One Sunday, after attending church, I went to a nearby park and wrote this poem.

Longing for Love

Living in a house with my family
Different noises everywhere
I feel so all alone
And yet no one seems to care.
Something is missing in my life
I've prayed and cried to God above,
About the little girl inside
That's been longing her whole life for love.
I've been mistreated and abused
By people that I thought loved me
The memories have kept me in bondage
Oh dear Lord, I'm crying out to thee!
I don't want to leave this earth
without being healed from this aching pain
The hurt is tearing me up inside
I need some sunshine, please stop the rain.
I'm so tired of being used
and taken for granted
Putting everyone else's feelings before mine
I won't keep living like this, I just can't!
Lord you said you wouldn't
put more on me than I can bear
Please God, send me a sign
Let me know that you really do care.
Lord you said to cast my cares upon you
I need you to show me how.
'Cause I've been carrying this burden,
for a very long time now.
I don't know how much more
of this loneliness I can take
Jesus, I am longing for love
Oh God, Please help me, for my own sake!
Dianna K. Cooper
Started Sunday, April 9, 2006
Finished Tuesday, April 18, 2006

In September of 2007, God opened a door for me to work at a college about one and a half hours away from where I lived. The day that my husband found out that I had gotten a job, was the day that I packed my van up with all my belongings and left him again. My daughter and I moved out. My oldest son was already attending the college where I had gotten a job, and was living on campus. My youngest son stayed with his dad.

After I moved, I begin to think about the friend I had years earlier; the one that I had an affair with. The devil knew I was lonely. He knew what my flesh wanted and enjoyed. James 4:7 says, *"Submit yourselves therefore unto God. Resist the devil, and he will flee from you."* Instead of me following after God's commandment, I followed my flesh. I called the guy's sister and questioned her about his whereabouts. I wanted to see him again!

I cannot tell you why my mind went back to him. I had not seen or heard from him in over 10 years. I just had this sudden urge to know how he was doing. I wanted to get in touch with him again and I knew in my heart that I would do it. I truly believe it was a trick of the enemy. 1 Peter 5:8 says, *"Be sober, be vigilant; because your adversary the devil, as a roaring lion, walketh about, seeking whom he may devour."* James 1:13-15 says, *"Let no man say when he is tempted, I am tempted of God: for God cannot be tempted with evil, neither tempteth he any man. But every man is tempted, when he is drawn away of his own lust, and enticed. Then when lust is conceived, it bringeth forth sin: and sin, when it is finished, bringeth forth death."*

One evening just after getting off work, my cell phone rang. It was my friend. Oh how wonderful it was to hear his voice again. He began to tell me about how he had changed and accepted Jesus in his life. What great news that was to my ears. He told me that he had gotten married, but he and his wife were separated and that she had since asked him for a divorce.

We began to talk on the phone every night before I went to bed. We would talk about the Bible. We would read scripture and pray together over the phone. Soon we planned to see each other face to face.

After a few weeks, I went to see him. He looked the same, only much more mature. As we begin to talk, he began to apologize, with tears in his eyes, for the way he treated me years before. He admitted to me that he was wrong and asked for my forgiveness. I then began to thank him and give him credit for boosting my self-esteem many years ago. We agreed that we would keep in touch and see each other every chance we could.

During one of my visits to see him, he told me that he wanted to move to the town where I lived. He went on to explain that he wanted to get away from his old surroundings. He had changed and didn't want to fall back into his old habits. He wanted to live by the straight and narrow this time.

So what did I do, I let him move in with me. Here I was again, "doing a friend a favor." He did not have a job, so he couldn't help me financially. Every day that I came home from work, my apartment had been cleaned and dinner was cooked. I was feeling good again. We had even talked about getting married. How could I plan to marry someone when we were both already married to someone else?

I had no business allowing that man to live in my apartment. Not only was he living there, but he was sleeping in my bed. Let me make one thing perfectly clear, he may have slept in my bed, but we did not have sex in any way the entire time he was living there, nor anytime thereafter. Thank God that did not happen. It was not by my strength, but only by the grace of God that it didn't happen. We both made it clearly understood that was not going to happen. But I give God all the credit for keeping me.

CHAPTER 20
BACK IN CHURCH

I had not been to church in a while now. Ironically, one of my work-study students invited me to her church. I was a little reluctant to go, but she told me that her pastor, a woman, had a television ministry as well. She gave me the information regarding the time and station to look for it. That night I went home and watched the service and made up my mind that I wanted to attend.

The following Sunday, my friend and I attended the church. Of course we walked into the church as if we were a married couple, knowing full well that we were not. At the end of the service, the pastor called both of us up to the front and prayed for us. She asked us what our names were, I'm not sure if she knew that we were not married. I don't remember any of the prayer she prayed for me that day. She did, however, tell my friend that he would find a job. She told him to talk with her husband when church was over and that he would help him. She gave me her number and asked me to give her a call.

A few days later, the pastor's husband helped my friend obtain a job. That was a relief for me financially. I was glad that he found employment and was able to start supporting himself instead of depending on me.

One evening, I decided to call the Pastor to talk with her. I told her all about my life and about how I was mistreated as a child. I explained to her about the raping and molestation I had endured as a child. I also told her about the letter I wrote to my step-brother and the outcome of it. I told her about the abuse I had encountered with my husband throughout my marriage. She would ask questions and I would give very detailed answers; she listened without interrupting.

Then she began to share with me about her past. She had endured some forms of abuse both in her childhood and adulthood as well. As she spoke, my eyes began to water. Finally, I had someone I could talk to who had experienced what I had and felt what I felt. I knew this had to be God! He had sent me some much-needed help at just the right time in my life. She prayed intently with

130

me. I asked and accepted God's forgiveness for what I had done to try and take revenge into my own hands.

My friend and I continued to attend the church together, but I began to feel convicted in my heart about him sleeping in my bed. I talked with him about it, and he moved out of my bedroom. But for me, that wasn't enough. I needed him to move out of my apartment, but my flesh wanted to continue to help him. I made excuses to myself to allow him to continue to stay.

One day while on the phone with the Pastor, she began to speak to me with authority in her voice. She told me that I was living in adultery. She told me not to let my good be evil spoken of and that my friend needed to move out of my apartment. I tried to explain to her that he didn't have anywhere to go. Once again, here I was making excuses. But she didn't accept what I told her. He needed to move out and that was that. I didn't know how I was going to tell him, but he had to leave; no more excuses.

Would you believe that later in that week when I got home, I had a notice on my apartment from my landlord? It stated that if a guest stayed with me for more than seven days and was not listed on the lease, that I was in direct violation of my lease and could face eviction. My friend had less than a week to move or I would lose my apartment. There was my answer!! God had given me a way of escape again! 1 Corinthians 10:13 says, *"There hath no temptation take you but such as is common to man: but God is faithful, who will not suffer you to be tempted above that ye are able; but will with the temptation also make a way to escape, the ye may be able to bear it."*

There was no discussion about my friend having to leave immediately. I didn't even have to initiate the conversation. God did it for me. I called the Pastor and told her about the notice I had gotten from my landlord. She informed me that she had a 14-room house and that my friend could stay in one of the rooms. She told him that he could stay in the house two months' rent free so he could get himself on the right track with his child support and any other legal fees he had to take care of.

My friend would still attend church, but our relationship shifted. I no longer saw him as someone I wanted to marry, but as my brother in Christ. However, he began to change. His old ways began to show back up again. He was falling back into the habits that he had run away from. My feelings toward him changed.

In February 2008, I became a member of the church. That was one of the best decisions I could have ever made. My Pastor took me under her wings and began to counsel me to help me to overcome my past. I began to see her as the Mother I never had. She was always straightforward with me in a loving manner. She gave me instructions and I was expected to follow them. I became submissive to her. I was obedient. I wanted to be healed. I was sick and tired of being sick and tired.

CHAPTER 21
My Breakthrough

One afternoon during a very stressful day at work, my blood pressure spiked really high. I drove myself to the hospital and was admitted. I called my husband and he immediately dropped everything and came to take care of my daughter and me.

While in the hospital, my Pastor and an Elder from the church came to visit me. My Pastor began to question me. She wanted to know what was on my mind and what could possibly be the cause of my blood pressure being elevated. I began to talk to her about my step-brother and how I was still upset about what happened. He was free as a bird and here I was still suffering over the abuse. I just couldn't understand why I was still dwelling on and thinking about him. I told her that all I wanted from him was a confession and an apology.

I remember the way she turned and looked at me. She said very sternly, "You will never get it. Isn't he married? Doesn't he have children of his own? Do you really think that he is going to mess up the good life he has now just to apologize and confess to you? You are wasting your life away waiting on an apology from him. You will always feel stuck as long as you are holding on to that. You must forgive him, forgive yourself, release the hurt and let it go."

"It's not fair for him to get away with what he did to me though," I said to her. "He doesn't care or even know what I am going through."

Then next thing she said to me was, "You will never be healed as long as you continue to hold on to wanting an apology from him." It was something about the tone of her voice that made the lights come on inside of me. You know what I'm talking about? It was like one of those "Aha" moments. I now realized that wanting an apology was holding me captive and tied to the hurt and the anger I felt towards my step-brother. I was in bondage because of what I wanted and felt I needed in order to move on. An apology from him was more than my forgiveness to him for what he had done to me. I had confessed the forgiveness with my mouth, but not accepted it in

134

my heart. Forgiveness was the key that would unlock the door to let my pain and my hurt, which I had been carrying for years, finally go free.

I was speechless; this was my answer! Forgiveness! I realized for the first time that I had to truly give it over to God and release myself. The answer was inside of me all the time.

Upon my release from the hospital, God used my Pastor to speak to me in a way that no one has ever spoken to me in my life. She began to speak life into me. She said to me, "Dianna, you were born for greatness. Quit living beneath that! You need to look in the mirror and tell God thank you. Be grateful for your life and get out of that pity party. Put all of the pain, the scars and the suffering into the Hands of God. He is bringing you to a place of healing. You have been living your present life based on your past. Ask God to dig up the root of your emotional turmoil and to go ahead and heal you. All of the thoughts you are having, give it to the Holy Ghost. Your destiny is already worked out; you need to pry your hands from trying to control it. Get over yourself. Your life is passing you by and you are wasting time dying over stuff. You are so tied up into your husband, your children and things until you have no relationship with God. You need to fall on your knees and find God. Learn how to stand. God is the only stable thing. You are a church-goer and not wrapped up in God."

She instilled in me all the virtues I needed, some of which my Grandmother started years earlier to make me whole again. My Pastor told me over and over again what a beautiful woman I was/am. She convinced me to believe that God loved me for me. She counseled me and told me that with God I am everything and without God I am nothing. With Gods' help, she put an end to that wounded little girl and brought out the beautiful woman I am today. I don't think she knows to this day, what a great impact she has had on my life.

I would be lying if I told you that the pain went away at that very moment, it did not. It took me totally surrendering my life to God and to His will for my life. I had to do much fasting and praying and asking God to work on me, to cleanse me, to heal me. I began to claim my healing, even though I didn't feel it. I began to thank God for my healing. Then I had to truly accept it.

Not only did I have to forgive my step-brother, I had to forgive my daddy and my step-mother as well. I had to forgive them all for the abuse, neglect and mistreatment that I suffered at their hands. I had to let it go completely and give it to God. The hatred and hurt I was holding in my heart was killing me; I didn't want to die.

I then had to go to my husband and ask him for forgiveness. I had to repent to him for my treatment towards him. I apologized for everything that I did or said to him that made him feel less than a man. I apologized to him for every single time I moved out on my own without him. He never left me; I either told him to leave or I left him. I apologized for trying to be "the boss" and living independent as a married woman.

We then had a family meeting with our children and asked for their forgiveness for not being the parents that we should have been to them. I had to apologize to them for not allowing my husband to be the head of the house as it was ordained by God. Finally, I had to forgive myself for holding on to the hurts of my past.

So, if you are holding on to the pain of your past, the key to your healing, as it was to mine, is FORGIVENESS. There must be forgiveness for your abuser(s); and most of all forgiveness for yourself.

Don't let another minute go by holding on to your past, let it go and give it to God. I am a living witness that you can and will be healed if you so desire.

AFTERWORD

Today, October 9, 2012 at 1:48 am, as I type the final words of my book…

I can truly say that I am FREE from the hurt and pain of my past and you can be too! I no longer feel any hurt or pain in those areas of my life.

Was it easy? No, it was not. But, if you truly want to be free, ask God to help you; and He will just as He did with me.

Do my abusers still lie on me? Sure they do. Do I still get tested in these areas? Yes. Do I want to get revenge on them? Sure I do. But instead, I continue to love and pray for them.

The Holy Spirit continues to keep me every single day of my life.

I have been with my husband 23 years. We have continued to have many rough patches and several more break-ups in our marriage. We have been through marriage counseling trying to overcome and deal with the issues of our marriage. We had to start over from the beginning and move forward. Look for my next book entitled, "The Purifying of the Fire".

My oldest son is out on his own and my youngest son and daughter are living at home with me and my husband. It has been a long road, but through it all, God gets all the glory.

Made in United States
Orlando, FL
12 March 2022

15686758R00078